Chocolate Lovers' Cookbook

PHOTOGRAPHY BY ROWAN FOTHERINGHAM
STYLING BY KAY FRANCIS

BayBooks
An imprint of HarperCollins*Publishers*

STOCKISTS

The Country Trader
122 Oxford Street
Paddington
Tel: (02) 331 7809

LA Decorative Design
15 Boundary Road
Rushcutters Bay
Tel: (02) 360 1493

The Bay Tree
40 Holdsworth Street
Woollahra
Tel: (02) 328 1101

Kitchen Kapers
74 Willoughby Road
Crows Nest
Tel: (02) 906 4655

Lifestyle Imports
159 Wyndham Street
Alexandria
Tel: (02) 319 5051

South Pacific Fabrics
15–19 Boundary Road
Rushcutters Bay
Tel: (02) 360 1199

A BAY BOOKS PUBLICATION
Bay Books, an imprint of
HarperCollins*Publishers*
25 Ryde Road, Pymble, Sydney NSW 2073, Australia
31 View Road, Glenfield, Auckland 10, New Zealand

First published in Australia in 1994

National Library of Australia
Cataloguing-in-Publication data:

The Chocolate Lovers' Cookbook
Rev. Ed.
ISBN 1 86378 150 1
1. Cookery (Chocolate).

641.6374
Printed by Griffin Press, Adelaide
Printed in Australia
9 8 7 6 5 4 3 2 1
97 96 95 94

Chapter openers and front cover photography by Rowan Fotheringham.
Chapter opener and front cover recipes and food stylist: Kay Francis.
Food stylist's assistant: Mino Francis.
Front cover recipe: Honeycomb Siena Cake (recipe page 17),
cake stand from The Country Trader, fabric from South Pacific Fabrics.

Contents

4
All About Chocolate

6
Cakes, Cookies and Slices

26
Desserts, Puddings and Ices

48
Gateaux

56
Pastries, Pies and Tarts

66
Homemade Confectionery

95
Index

All About Chocolate

Chocolate is one of life's great pleasures. Its rich consistency and distinctive flavour appeal to almost everyone's sweet tooth. It is also a prime source of instant energy as it is full of carbohydrate and contains traces of the stimulants caffeine and theobromine.

This book teaches you all about how to make your own handmade chocolates with individual illustrations, step-by-step recipes and easy-to-follow methods. There are simple recipes for beginners, or you can make more sophisticated chocolates to round off a special occasion with real style. And there are chocolate cakes, including recipes for flourless cakes, biscuits, gâteaux, and every kind of exotic dessert.

Chocolate was first brought to the western world 400 years ago, when Spanish explorers came across it in South America. At first it was only used as a drink, but in the last century the familiar chocolate bar was invented in Switzerland and quickly became the world's most popular confection.

The tree that yields chocolate is aptly named *Theobroma*, which means 'food of the gods'. The tree has been cultivated for so many centuries that there are probably no wild trees left, and it is from the pale purple-pink beans within the pulp of the hanging fruit that chocolate is made. The beans are fermented, dried, roasted and processed into a paste called chocolate liquor. Chocolate liquor is richly coloured and bitter and not generally available, as it is difficult to cook with.

Cocoa powder is made by pressing cocoa butter (vegetable fat) out of the pure chocolate liquor and then pulverising the remains. Extra cocoa butter has to be added to chocolate liquor to turn it into block chocolate. Cocoa has less fat and sugar than block chocolate, but also less of the true chocolate flavour.

The less sweet, good-quality dark or plain chocolate blocks are satisfactory for cooking, or you can use a good-quality cooking chocolate. Chocolate with a fairly high cocoa butter content has more fluidity and won't ball around the spoon when melting. Thick, chunky chocolate may not melt quite as easily as thinner blocks, but some cooking chocolate is labelled easy-to-melt. If chocolate is not melting easily, add a little copha fat (2 to 3 per cent of weight of chocolate). This increases the snap quality of the chocolate so a chocolate coating on a cake may not cut quite so neatly.

How to Make the Most of Chocolate

Chocolate Drinks

For chocolate-flavoured liquid (ie hot or cold chocolate drinks), allow 125 g (4 oz) chocolate per 4 cups (1 litre/35 fl oz) of liquid. Chop the chocolate into the liquid and allow it to melt slowly over a low heat. The result will be a deliciously thick and velvety mixture.

You can substitute 60 g (2 oz) cocoa powder and 40 g (1½ oz) sugar per 100 g (3½ oz) chocolate if you prefer.

If you wish to drink the chocolate mixture cold, bear in mind that it will thicken considerably as it cools down.

Chocolate Custard

Melt the chocolate in the milk as it heats and proceed as usual.

Grating Chocolate

Before grating chocolate, place it in the fridge for an hour or so. Grate the chocolate onto a piece of kitchen paper so it can be weighed easily as you go along. Do not touch grated chocolate — it will melt immediately with the warmth of your hand.

Chopping Chocolate

The easiest way to chop chocolate is to first break the slab into smallish pieces on a large board. Press down on the back of the blade as you chop.

Chocolate and Cream

To melt chocolate in fresh cream, put the cream in a heavy-based saucepan and heat on a very low flame. Add pieces of chocolate and stir until just melted. Allow to cool and then beat by hand or with an electric beater. The cream will double in volume and become rich and light in texture. Use immediately, before it hardens, to cover cakes or desserts.

Cooking with Chocolate

- When a recipe requires melted chocolate, it must be heated in a bowl or on a plate suspended over (but definitely not in) a pan of hot, but not boiling, water. Over-heated chocolate has a bitter taste and loses its glossy shine and delicious aroma.
- Melt chocolate slowly without stirring. Some cooks advocate working it with a palette knife if it is to be used for coating cakes or making chocolate cases because that helps to keep the gloss when it sets. The chocolate should be no more than lukewarm.
- Chop or break chocolate into small pieces before melting so it melts quickly and evenly. Do not stir chocolate while it melts.
- To test that chocolate is melted, dip the point of a knife into the centre.
- Cool chocolate at room temperature. This also helps to maintain the gloss.
- Make sure that not even a drop of water gets into the bowl (unless this is part of the recipe). Water prevents a good sheen and will make the chocolate thick.
- Remember that drinking chocolate and cocoa are not exactly interchangeable: drinking chocolate has a milder, sweeter flavour.

Storing Handmade Chocolates

- Do not refrigerate handmade chocolates or they will discolour and sweat when you remove them from fridge.
- The handmade chocolates in this book will keep for 2 to 3 weeks, but those made with cream have a shorter shelf life. However, it is unlikely that anything as tempting as handmade chocolates will last long in the cupboard!

Cakes, Cookies and Slices

For those times when you need something to nibble on SOON! These don't need too many fancy ingredients, don't take too much time, and will make you very popular with your family and friends.

Wire rack from The Bay Tree

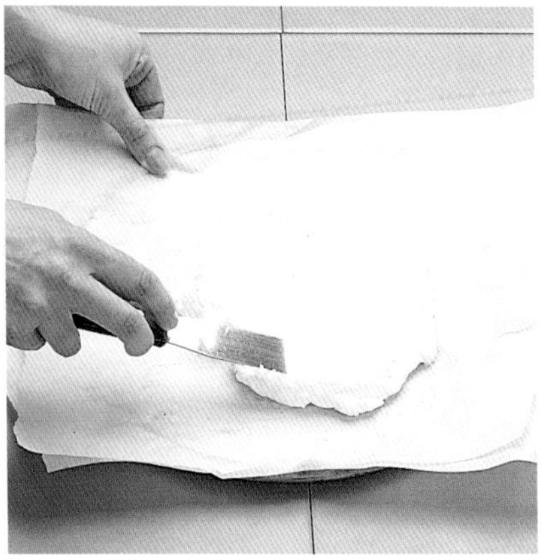

Spread the meringue mixture in circles.

Add the cooled chocolate mixture to the cream.

Spread each meringue with the chocolate cream.

Pictured on previous pages: Date Fudge Slice (page 11), Double Chocolate Chip Brownies (page 18)

CHOCOLATE DELUXE

This cake should be filled at least 2 to 3 hours before serving. It can be made the day before and kept in the refrigerator overnight. This will ensure that the meringue is soft enough to cut.

- ***4 egg whites***
- ***220 g (7 oz) caster sugar***
- ***250 g (8 oz) dark or cooking chocolate***
- ***½ cup (125 ml/4 fl oz) water***
- ***2½ cups (625 ml/21 fl oz) thickened cream***
- ***60 g (2 oz) extra chocolate, melted***

Preheat the oven to 130°C (250°F).

Line 3 baking sheets with non-stick baking paper and mark three 20 to 23 cm (8 to 9 in) circles on the paper.

Whisk egg whites until stiff, add half the sugar and whisk until stiff and glossy. Fold in remaining sugar. Spread mixture over the marked circles and bake for about 1 hour, until dry.

Break chocolate into small pieces and place them in a small pan with water. Melt over gentle heat, then cool.

Whip cream until it begins to thicken, then add cool chocolate mixture and continue to beat until thick.

Spread each meringue round with chocolate cream and layer one on top of the other. Spread top and sides with mixture, reserving some for decoration, and leave it to stand for 2 to 3 hours. Decorate cake with some of the reserved chocolate mixture, piped, and drizzle extra chocolate over the top.

SERVES 6 TO 8

Chocolate Deluxe

CHOCOLATE CASES

250 g (8 oz) dark or cooking chocolate

125 g (4 oz) margarine or butter

110 g (3½ oz) caster sugar

2 eggs

125 g (4 oz) self-raising flour

90 g (3 oz) strawberry jam, warmed

1 tablespoon curaçao

½ cup (125 ml/4 fl oz) cream

12 strawberries, washed

Preheat the oven to 190°C (375°F).

Melt chocolate in a bowl set over a pan of hot water. Spread chocolate on 2 large sheets of waxed paper, to make level rectangles of 14 x 18 cm (5½ x 7 in). Leave to set. Cut each sheet into 24 squares, 4.5 cm (1¾ in) square, using a hot, wet knife.

In a bowl, cream margarine or butter with sugar until light and fluffy. Add eggs, beating well after each addition, and then gradually fold in sifted flour.

Grease a 29 x 19 cm (11½ x 7½ in) lamington tin and line the base with greaseproof paper. Spread cake mixture into tin and bake for about 20 minutes. Cool on a wire rack.

Cut cake in half widthways and trim ½ cm (¼ in) from both short sides and from 1 long side, so that cake can be cut into even squares. Sandwich the 2 pieces of cake with half the strawberry jam. Sprinkle with curaçao.

Cut cake into 12 squares, each 4.5 cm (1¾ in). Spread rest of jam thinly on sides .of cake squares. Stick a chocolate square onto each of the 4 sides of the cakes.

Whip cream until it is stiff and pipe a swirl of cream on top of each chocolate case. Place one strawberry on top of each cake.

Note: Chocolate cases can be varied with other flavours. For example, fill with a layer of cherry jam, sprinkle with kirsch, and top with a fresh cherry; or fill with marmalade, sprinkle with Grand Marnier and top with an orange slice or candied orange peel.

MAKES 12

CHOCOLATE LAYER CAKE

125 g (4 oz) butter

110 g (3½ oz) caster sugar

1 tablespoon cocoa powder dissolved in 2 tablespoons boiling water

2 large eggs

few drops vanilla essence

100 g (3½ oz) self-raising flour, sifted

1¼ cups (310 ml/10 fl oz) cream

DECORATION

45 g (1½ oz) butter, at room temperature

75 g (2½ oz) icing sugar

1 teaspoon cocoa powder

½ teaspoon boiling water

Preheat the oven to 190°C (375°F).

Cream butter and sugar together for 5 minutes until light and creamy. Stir in cocoa liquid.

Lightly beat together eggs and vanilla essence. Add to creamed mixture a little at a time, beating well after each addition. Add a little sifted flour with the last addition of egg. Using a metal spoon, fold in remaining flour.

Spoon mixture into 2 greased and lined 18 cm (7 in) sandwich tins and bake on middle shelf of oven for 20 to 25 minutes. Turn cakes out onto a rack to cool.

While cake cools, whip cream until it forms peaks. Sandwich cake with half whipped cream and spread the rest over the top.

To Prepare the Decoration: Cream together butter and icing sugar until light and fluffy. Dissolve cocoa in water and blend it with buttercream. Fit a piping bag with a small plain icing nozzle and fill it with chocolate buttercream. Pipe cream in parallel lines over top of cake.

Note: To make chocolate walnut cake, add chopped walnuts to cake mixture. Mix 110 g (3½ oz) chopped walnuts with beaten eggs (omit vanilla essence) before beating them into the creamed butter and sugar. Decorate the top of the cake with walnut halves or grated chocolate instead of piped chocolate buttercream.

SERVES 6 TO 8

MELTING CHOCOLATE CONVENTIONALLY

Melt chocolate slowly without stirring. Some cooks advocate working it with a palette knife if the chocolate is to be used for coating cakes or making chocolate cases — this helps to keep the gloss when the chocolate sets. The chocolate should be no more than lukewarm when melted.

MELTING CHOCOLATE IN A MICROWAVE

To melt chocolate in the microwave, place chocolate, broken into small pieces, in a bowl and heat on Medium/High for 1 minute. Stir, then repeat, stirring after each minute. Take care not to overheat as chocolate burns easily.

VIENNA CAKE

- *175 g (6 oz) flour*
- *1 teaspoon baking powder*
- *½ teaspoon bicarbonate of soda*
- *50 g (2 oz) cocoa powder*
- *100 g (3½ oz) butter*
- *225 g (7 oz) soft dark brown sugar*
- *2 eggs*
- *80 ml (2½ fl oz) yoghurt*

Icing and Filling

- *100 g (3½ oz) butter, at room temperature*
- *150 g (5 oz) icing sugar*
- *few drops vanilla essence*
- *2 teaspoons cocoa powder*
- *1 tablespoon rum*
- *150 ml (5 fl oz) thickened cream*
- *8 thin chocolate triangles (see recipe for Chocolate Cases, page 10, and follow the method for chocolate squares)*

Preheat the oven to 190°C (375°F).

Sift together flour, baking powder and bicarbonate of soda. Mix cocoa with a little hot water to form a smooth paste.

In a bowl, cream butter and sugar until light and fluffy. Beat in eggs, yoghurt, cocoa paste and, finally, flour mixture. Pour into a greased and base-lined 20 cm (8 in) square cake tin. Bake for 35 minutes. Cool in tin for 10 minutes, then turn onto a wire rack.

To Make the Icing: Beat butter with icing sugar and vanilla essence until very light and fluffy. Fold in cocoa and rum.

In another bowl, beat cream until stiff. When cake is cold, cut it into 3 horizontal layers, and sandwich them together with whipped cream. Spread chocolate buttercream on top and decorate with chocolate triangles.

SERVES 8

TOSCANAS

- *125 g (4 oz) self-raising flour*
- *100 g (3½ oz) ground almonds*
- *85 g (3 oz) brown sugar*
- *125 g (4 oz) melted butter*
- *75 g (2½ oz) dark or cooking chocolate*

Topping

- *6 tablespoons cream*
- *140 g (4½ oz) butter*
- *7 tablespoons caster sugar*
- *4 tablespoons golden syrup*
- *35 g (1 oz) flaked almonds*

Preheat the oven to 200°C (400°F).

Combine flour and ground almonds, add sugar and melted butter. Mix well.

Spread mixture in a greased lamington tin and bake for 10 to 12 minutes. Cool.

To Prepare the Topping: Place cream, butter, sugar and golden syrup in a heavy-based saucepan. Gently bring to the boil and cook, stirring for 10 minutes. Add almonds and, still stirring, simmer for 5 minutes.

Lower oven temperature to 190°C (375°F). Spread topping over cooled biscuit. Return to the oven for 15 minutes. Cool and cut into different shapes.

Melt chocolate in a bowl over a pan of hot water. Dip base of each biscuit in chocolate and leave to set.

MAKES ABOUT 18

DATE FUDGE SLICE

- *250 g (8 oz) butter*
- *340 g (11 oz) brown sugar*
- *4 tablespoons cocoa*
- *⅓ cup (80 ml/2½ fl oz) treacle*
- *2 eggs, beaten*
- *315 g (10½ oz) wholemeal self-raising flour*
- *155 g (5 oz) dates, chopped*
- *125 g (4 oz) walnuts, chopped*

Icing

- *60 g (2 oz) dark or cooking chocolate*
- *2 tablespoons water*
- *1 teaspoon oil*
- *235 g (7½ oz) icing sugar, sifted*

Preheat the oven to 180°C (350°F).

Combine butter, sugar, cocoa and treacle in a large saucepan. Melt, stirring, over low heat. Cool. Mix in egg and then remaining ingredients. Pour into a greased and lined 25 x 30 x 5 cm (10 x 12 x 2 in) baking tin and bake on centre shelf of oven for 25 minutes, or until centre feels firm. Cool in the tin.

To Prepare the Icing: Combine chocolate, water and oil in a bowl positioned over a saucepan of simmering water. Stir until smooth, then beat in icing sugar. Keep warm.

Turn fudge out onto a board. Pour icing over, spreading it right to the edge. When set, cut fudge into slices.

MAKES ABOUT 24 SLICES

MELTING CHOCOLATE

If your chocolate is not melting easily, add a little copha (about 2 or 3 per cent of the weight of the chocolate). This can increase the 'snap' quality of the chocolate so that a chocolate coating on a cake may not cut quite so neatly.

DEVIL'S FOOD CAKE WITH FUDGE FILLING

280 g (9 oz) self-raising flour
385 g (12½ oz) caster sugar
1 teaspoon bicarbonate soda
65 g (2 oz) cocoa
150 g (5 oz) butter, at room temperature
1 teaspoon vanilla
1 cup (250 ml/8 fl oz) water
3 eggs

FUDGE

300 g (10 oz) raw sugar
2 tablespoons golden syrup
90 g (3 oz) unsalted butter
60 g (2 oz) cocoa
1¼ cups (310 ml/10 fl oz) water

Preheat the oven to 180°C (350°F).

Sift dry ingredients into a large bowl. Add butter, vanilla and water. Beat for three minutes, then add eggs, one at a time, beating after each addition. Beat for three minutes. Pour into 2 buttered, base-lined and lightly-floured 20 to 23 cm (8 to 9 in) cake tins. Bake for 35 minutes, or until centre of cakes spring back when lightly touched. Cool in tins.

To Prepare the Fudge: Combine all ingredients in a large heavy-based saucepan and cook over a low heat, stirring frequently until sugar has dissolved. Increase heat and boil until temperature reaches 114°C (238°F) on a sugar thermometer, or until fudge stage is reached. Do not stir mixture, but occasionally draw a wooden spoon across the bottom of the pan, and the sugar thermometer across the top. Remove from heat.

To Assemble the Cake: Cut each cake in half horizontally. Place one top portion (cut side up) on a serving plate and spread with a little warm fudge, using a large metal spatula. Top with base half (cut side down) and spread fudge again. Top with base portion from remaining cake, cut side up, and spread with fudge. Place remaining cake layer on top (cut side down) and spread remaining fudge over the top and around the sides as well. To serve, cut cake with a hot sharp knife. (This cake is best made the day before, to allow fudge to soften a little before cutting. Stand it, covered, at room temperature.)

SERVES 10 TO 12

MARBLE CAKE

185 g (6 oz) margarine or butter
185 g (6 oz) caster sugar
3 large eggs
160 g (5 oz) plain flour
120 g (4 oz) self-raising flour
1 tablespoon cocoa powder
a little milk
orange and yellow food colourings
finely grated rind 1 orange
1 teaspoon orange juice
finely grated rind 1 lemon
1 teaspoon lemon juice
few drops vanilla essence

Preheat the oven to 180°C (350°F).

Grease and flour a 20 cm (8 in) ring cake tin.

Place margarine or butter and sugar in a mixer bowl and, with mixer at high speed, cream until light and fluffy. Add eggs, one at a time, beating well. Sift flours together and fold into mixture with a large metal spoon.

Divide mixture into 4 portions. Mix cocoa powder and 1 teaspoon milk into one portion. Add orange rind and juice to second portion, with a few drops of orange colouring. Add lemon rind and juice to third portion with a few drops of yellow colouring. Add vanilla to last portion.

Place spoonfuls of mixture alternately in prepared cake tin. Bake for 35 to 45 minutes, until cake is well risen and firm to the touch. Remove from oven and cool slightly. Turn out onto a wire rack to complete cooling.

SERVES 8

ZEST

The outer layer of citrus fruit skin is known as zest. It may be removed by using a grater (ensure only the colour of the skin is removed, as the white pith underneath is bitter) or may be peeled off using a vegetable peeler. These pieces of skin may be sliced thinly, blanched and used in recipes. A zester will make even finer strips and this peel does not require blanching.

Marble Cake

FLORENTINES

90 g (3 oz) butter

110 g (3½ oz) caster sugar

100 g (3½ oz) chopped almonds

2 tablespoons chopped sultanas

5 glacé cherries, chopped

2 tablespoons chopped mixed peel, re-chopped

1 tablespoon cream

100 g (3½ oz) dark chocolate

Preheat the oven to 180°C (350°F).

Line baking sheets with non-stick paper. Melt butter, add the sugar and boil for 1 minute. Stir in remaining ingredients, except chocolate, and mix well. Drop mixture in small heaps onto baking sheets, keeping them well apart. Bake for 10 minutes, or until golden brown.

Remove biscuits from oven and press edges to a neat shape. When they begin to firm, transfer them to a rack and cool.

Melt chocolate in a bowl over a pan of hot water. Allow to cool until fairly thick. Spread backs of biscuits thickly with chocolate. Using a fork, mark chocolate with wavy lines and leave it to set.

MAKES ABOUT 14

PEAR AND CHOCOLATE SPONGE

175 g (6 oz) butter or margarine

175 g (6 oz) caster sugar

3 eggs

175 g (6 oz) self-raising flour

4 tablespoons walnuts, chopped

12 canned pear halves, drained

30 g (1 oz) dark or cooking chocolate, melted

7 walnut halves

Chocolate Buttercream

225 g (7 oz) icing sugar, sieved

225 g (7 oz) butter, at room temperature

4 teaspoons cocoa powder

½ teaspoon boiling water

few drops vanilla essence

Preheat the oven to 190°C (375°F).

Cream butter or margarine and caster sugar until light and fluffy, then beat in eggs, one at a time, adding a spoonful of flour with each. Sieve remaining flour and fold in with a metal spoon.

Divide mixture between two greased and lined 20 cm (8 in) sandwich tins. Bake for 25 to 30 minutes. Turn cake out and cool it on a wire rack.

To Make Chocolate Buttercream: Beat icing sugar with butter until light and fluffy. Dissolve cocoa in water, and stir this into butter and sugar with vanilla essence.

Split each sponge in half. Spread ⅓ of buttercream on 3 of the halves. Thinly slice 6 pear halves and lay them on top of buttercream. Sandwich together, with plain sponge on top.

Spread top and sides of cake with remaining buttercream. Press chopped nuts onto sides. Arrange remaining 6 pear halves on top and drizzle with melted chocolate. Decorate with walnut halves.

SERVES 8

MELTING CHOCOLATE

Chocolate with a fairly high cocoa butter content has more fluidity and won't ball around the spoon when melting.

Sieve the flour and fold it in with a metal spoon.

Divide the mixture between greased, lined tins.

Blend the cocoa with a little boiling water and stir it into the butter and sugar.

Pear and Chocolate Sponge

Glass cake stand from The Country Trader, fabric from South Pacific Fabrics

HONEYCOMB SIENA CAKE

60 g (2 oz) dried apricots, sliced

125 ml (4 fl oz) brandy

90 g (3 oz) roasted slivered almonds, roughly chopped

125 g (4 oz) roasted hazelnuts, roughly chopped

300 g (10 oz) glacé figs, sliced

85 g (3 oz) plain flour

2 tablespoons cocoa

1 teaspoon cinnamon

85 g (3 oz) raw sugar

180 g (6 oz) honey

125 g (4 oz) dark or cooking chocolate, melted

200 g (6½ oz) honeycomb, cut into 1 cm (½ in) cubes

icing sugar for dusting

Preheat the oven to 160°C (325°F).

Soak apricots in brandy for at least 1 hour, preferably longer.

Combine almonds, hazelnuts, figs, flour, cocoa and cinnamon.

In a large saucepan, heat sugar and honey, stirring until sugar has dissolved. Boil, without stirring, for about 5 minutes, or until syrup forms a soft ball when a small amount is dropped into a glass of cold water.

Remove from heat, stir in nut mixture, chocolate, honeycomb, apricots and brandy. Spoon into a 20 cm (8 in) greased and base-lined pan, smoothing the top. Bake for 40 to 45 minutes. Cool in tin for 30 minutes, turn onto a wire rack and peel off base paper while cake is still warm. Cool, then dust cake generously with icing sugar. Wrap cake in foil and refrigerate until required. Serve in thin wedges or small squares.

SERVES 10 TO 12

Honeycomb Siena Cake

FLOURLESS MOCHA MACADAMIA CAKE

250 g (8 oz) raw sugar

1 tablespoon instant espresso coffee powder

60 ml (2 fl oz) water

250 g (8 oz) dark or cooking chocolate, broken into pieces

1 teaspoon almond essence

125 g (4 oz) unsalted butter, at room temperature

8 eggs, separated

90 g (3 oz) roasted macadamia nuts, finely ground

ICING

250 g (8 oz) dark or cooking chocolate

1 tablespoon instant espresso coffee powder

60 ml (2 fl oz) water

250 g (8 oz) unsalted butter, at room temperature

3 egg yolks

155 g (5 oz) icing sugar, sifted

15 g (½ oz) roasted macadamia nuts

Preheat the oven to 180°C (350°F).

Heat together sugar, coffee powder and water in a saucepan, stirring, until sugar has dissolved. Remove from heat and stir in chocolate and almond essence until chocolate has melted and mixture is smooth. Cool.

Beat butter until light and fluffy. Add egg yolks, one at a time, beating well after each addition. Stir in chocolate mixture, then macadamias.

Beat egg whites until stiff but not dry. Stir ¼ of egg whites into chocolate mixture, then gently fold in remainder. Pour mixture into 2 buttered, base-lined and lightly-floured 23 cm (9 in) cake tins. Bake in centre of oven for 30 minutes, or until cakes spring back when lightly touched in the centre. Cool in tins.

To Prepare the Icing: Heat chocolate and coffee powder and water in a small saucepan, stirring, until smooth. Cool. Beat butter with an electric mixer until pale and fluffy. Add egg yolks one at a time, beating well after each addition. Beat in chocolate mixture, then icing sugar, until smooth. Refrigerate until thick enough to spread.

To Assemble the Cake: Place one layer on a serving plate and spread top with icing. Place second cake layer on this and spread remaining icing on top and sides. Decorate with macadamias. Refrigerate until required.

SERVES 10 TO 12

CHOCOLATE FUDGIES

125 g (4 oz) butter

315 g (10½ oz) brown sugar

2 eggs

160 g (5 oz) flour, sifted

3 to 4 tablespoons sifted cocoa powder

few drops vanilla essence

125 g (4 oz) chopped walnuts

2 tablespoons icing sugar

Preheat the oven to 180°C (350°F).

In a large bowl, cream butter and sugar until light and fluffy. Add eggs, one at a time, beating continually.

Fold in sifted flour and cocoa powder, then add vanilla and chopped nuts. Continue to mix until thoroughly blended.

Drop teaspoonfuls of mixture on a greased baking sheet. Dust with icing sugar. Bake for about 12 minutes. Cool on a wire rack and serve.

MAKES ABOUT 48

DOUBLE CHOCOLATE CHIP BROWNIES

125 g (4 oz) unsalted butter

60 g (2 oz) dark or cooking chocolate

250 g (8 oz) raw sugar

60 g (2 oz) self-raising flour, sifted

60 g (2 oz) pecans or walnuts, chopped

1 teaspoon vanilla essence

2 eggs, slightly beaten

185 g (6 oz) chocolate chips

Preheat the oven to 180°C (350°F).

Melt butter and chocolate in the top of a double boiler or in a microwave. Combine with sugar, flour, nuts and vanilla in a large bowl, stirring with a wooden spoon. Mix in eggs, then chocolate chips.

Pour mixture into a greased and base-lined 20 cm (8 in) square cake tin. Bake for 30 to 40 minutes, or until a skewer inserted in the centre of the cake comes out clean. Cool in tin for 5 minutes, then, with a metal spatula, cut around edge of cake to separate it from tin. Turn out onto a board and peel off baking paper while cake is warm. Cool and cut into 5 cm (2 in) squares.

MAKES 16

Double Chocolate Chip Brownies

GRATING CHOCOLATE

Grate chocolate onto a piece of kitchen paper so it can be weighed easily. Do not touch grated chocolate, because it will melt immediately from the warmth of your hand.

CHOCOLATE CHIP COOKIES

125 g (4 oz) butter
60 g (2 oz) sugar
85 g (3 oz) brown sugar
1 egg
125 g (4 oz) plain flour
125 g (4 oz) self-raising flour
½ teaspoon salt
½ teaspoon bicarbonate of soda
grated rind 1 orange
140 g (4½ oz) chocolate chips or chocolate drops
60 g (2 oz) chopped walnuts

Preheat the oven to 190°C (375°F).

Chocolate Chip Cookies

Cream butter, sugar and brown sugar together until light and fluffy. Add egg and beat thoroughly.

Sift flours, salt and bicarbonate of soda into mixture and beat. Stir in orange rind, chocolate chips or drops, and nuts.

Grease a baking sheet. Roll teaspoonfuls of mixture into balls, place them on baking sheet and press with a fork.

Bake for about 10 minutes until golden brown. Cool and serve.

MAKES ABOUT 48

CHOCOLATE DELIGHTS

345 g (11 oz) dark or cooking chocolate
1¼ cups (310 ml/10 fl oz) cream
grated rind 1 orange
50 g (2 oz) cocoa powder

Grate chocolate. Place cream in a small pan and bring it to the boil. Tip in grated chocolate and stir well over a gentle heat until it is completely melted and forms a smooth paste. Remove from heat.

Continue to stir until cooled. Stir in grated orange rind, then leave in a cool place (preferably not the refrigerator) for 24 hours.

Pour cocoa onto a plate and, using 2 teaspoons, scoop out small amounts of chocolate cream and roll into smooth balls. Roll each ball in cocoa and serve immediately — do not keep too long or cream will turn sour.

MAKES 550 G

SACHER TORTE

250 g (8 oz) chocolate

150 g (5 oz) butter, at room temperature

150 g (5 oz) caster sugar

6 eggs, separated

150 g (5 oz) self-raising flour

2 tablespoons apricot jam, warmed

a little coffee glacé icing (see recipe for chocolate glacé icing page 24)

Covering

200 g (6½ oz) chocolate

2 tablespoons copha

Preheat the oven to 180°C (350°F).

Break chocolate into squares and place in bowl over a pan of just simmering water, over low heat. Leave until softened, but not melted.

Blend softened chocolate and butter with a wooden spoon. Add sugar and mix well.

Sacher Torte

Mix in egg yolks, one at a time, and beat until blended.

In another bowl, beat egg whites until stiff. Fold egg whites and flour alternately into chocolate mixture, finishing with egg white. Be careful not to overmix or beat the mixture.

Pour into 2 greased and floured 20 cm (8 in) cake tins. Bake for 45 to 60 minutes, until top springs bac when lightly touched. Leave in tins overnight.

The following day, turn out the cakes. Spread warmed jam over each cake, then sandwich cake halves.

To Make the Covering: Break chocolate into a bowl and melt with copha over a pan of hot water. Stir gently until it dissolves, then pour onto cake and spread quickly with a metal spatula to completely cover cake. Allow to set.

Decorate with the words 'Sacher Torte' piped in coffee glacé icing.

SERVES 6 TO 8

LAMINGTONS

175 g (6 oz) butter

175 g (6 oz) caster sugar

3 eggs

250 g (8 oz) self-raising flour

⅔ cup (150 ml/5 fl oz) milk

½ teaspoon vanilla essence

Icing

25 g (1 oz) butter

¼ cup (60 ml/2 fl oz) boiling water

2 tablespoons cocoa powder

275 g (9 oz) icing sugar

180 g (6 oz) desiccated coconut

Two days before you make lamingtons, make the cake.

Preheat the oven to 180°C (350°F).

To Prepare the Cake: Cream butter and sugar until light and fluffy. Gradually add eggs, beating well after each addition. Alternately fold in flour and milk, and stir in vanilla essence.

Place mixture in a greased, lined lamington tin and bake for 30 to 35 minutes. Cool cake on a wire rack. Wrap and store cake for 2 days, then cut it into 6 cm (2½ in) cubes.

To Prepare the Icing: Place butter in a bowl and pour in boiling water. Add cocoa and, beating continuously, gradually add icing sugar. Place bowl of icing over a pan of hot water. Using a long-pronged fork to hold the cubes of cake, dip each piece into the icing and roll it immediately in desiccated coconut. Leave lamingtons to set.

MAKES APPROXIMATELY 24

LUCERNES

50 g (2 oz) dark or cooking chocolate

225 g (7 oz) self-raising flour, sieved

125 g (4 oz) soft margarine

220 g (7 oz) caster sugar

4 beaten eggs

Filling

1 tablespoon powdered gelatine

2 cups (500 ml/16 fl oz) whipped cream

few glacé cherries, halved or chopped

Decoration

1¼ cups (310 ml/10 fl oz) thickened cream

chopped walnuts, slivered almonds or grated chocolate

Preheat the oven to 200°C (400°F).

Grease, line with greaseproof paper and grease again two 30 x 25 cm (12 x 10 in) swiss roll tins. Melt chocolate in a bowl set over a pan of hot water.

Place all other cake ingredients together in a large mixing bowl and beat well for 4 to 5 minutes until thoroughly blended and creamy. Add melted chocolate and mix in. Spread mixture smoothly over bases of tins. Bake for 10 to 12 minutes until firm to the touch. Turn out and cool on a wire rack.

Trim hard edges from cooled sponges and level them with a sharp knife. Cut one sponge in half lengthways. Reserve one half and cut remaining half into 2 pieces lengthways, one of which should be twice as wide as the other (2:1). You should now have 3 slices cut from that one sponge layer, each a little narrower than the last, plus one whole sponge layer.

To Make the Filling: Soften gelatine in a little cold water, then dissolve over a saucepan of hot water. Cool. Add the cream and whip until stiff. Fold through glacé cherries.

Sandwich cut sponge layers with cream mixture, arranging layers with the largest at the bottom. Pile more whipped cream mixture on top and sides to form a smooth-sided triangular shape.

Cut reserved whole sponge in half lengthways. Score one side of each piece with a knife. Turn pieces over and spread unscored side with remaining cream filling. Place each strip, filling-side down, on either side of the long triangle, enclosing the filling and meeting in a point at the top. Make sure side pieces are resting on the jutting-out base of the triangle.

Whip cream (for decoration) until stiff and spread it over the outer long sides. Sprinkle sides with chopped nuts or grated chocolate.

Note: For variety, you can flavour lucernes with orange or lemon juice and grated rind, or try a few drops of peppermint essence and green food colouring. For a pretty pastel pink cream, mix in a few drops of cochineal.

MAKES ABOUT 12 SLICES

CHOCOLATE CHESTNUT CAKE

- *125 g (4 oz) margarine or butter*
- *110 g (3½ oz) caster sugar*
- *2 eggs*
- *125 g (4 oz) self-raising flour*
- *25 g (1 oz) cocoa powder*
- *440 g (14 oz) canned chestnut purée*
- *1 tablespoon rum*
- *75 g (2½ oz) icing sugar*

Icing

- *125 g (4 oz) dark or cooking chocolate*
- *3 tablespoons water*
- *1 teaspoon unflavoured vegetable oil*
- *2 tablespoons caster sugar*

Preheat the oven to 190°C (375°F).

Grease a 20 cm (8 in) cake tin and line it with greaseproof paper.

Cream margarine or butter with sugar until light and fluffy. Add eggs gradually, beating all the time. Sift together flour and cocoa powder and gradually fold them into mixture. Pour mixture into the cake tin and bake for 20 to 25 minutes until top is firm and cake pulls back from the sides of the pan. Cool in tin for 10 minutes then turn out onto a rack.

Cut cake into three equal layers horizontally. In a bowl, beat together chestnut purée, rum and icing sugar. Spread this mixture on 2 layers of cake, then sandwich all layers together.

In a pan over low heat, melt together chocolate, water, oil and sugar. Stir well to blend thoroughly. Cool until mixture is quite thick, but not set. Pour over cake, spreading evenly with a metal spatula. Leave in a cool place to set before serving.

Note: Cake can be decorated with chocolate leaves. Melt dark chocolate in a double boiler. Allow to cool slightly. Using a small teaspoon or spatula, carefully spread chocolate on undersides of washed and dried firm leaves (eg camellias). Allow to set at room temperature. Carefully peel leaf from chocolate, starting at the stem end.

SERVES 6 TO 8

CHOCOLATE VIENNESE

275 g (9 oz) butter, at room temperature

75 g (2½ oz) caster sugar

50 g (2 oz) dark or cooking chocolate, melted

265 g (8½ oz) flour

4 tablespoons cocoa powder

65 g (2 oz) ground almonds

FILLING

50 g (2 oz) margarine or butter

75 g (2½ oz) icing sugar

1 teaspoon cocoa powder

50 g (2 oz) dark or cooking chocolate, melted

Preheat the oven to 180°C (350°F).

Cream butter, sugar and melted chocolate.

Sieve flour with cocoa powder and fold into mixture with ground almonds. Transfer mixture to a piping bag fitted with a 1 cm (½ in) star nozzle and pipe 20 whirls and 20 fingers onto a greased baking sheet.

This is a very stiff mixture so extra pressure is needed to pipe it.

Bake for 10 to 15 minutes. Cool on a wire rack.

To Make the Filling: Cream margarine or butter with sugar until light. Blend cocoa with a little boiling water and mix with creamed mixture. Use to sandwich the whirls and fingers in pairs.

Place cooled melted chocolate in a small plastic bag, snip one corner and squeeze chocolate over biscuits in a decorative pattern.

MAKES 20

MELTING CHOCOLATE

Chop or break chocolate into small pieces before you melt it, so it will melt quickly and evenly. Do not stir the chocolate while it is melting. Test that the chocolate is melted by dipping the point of a knife into the centre.

CHOCOLATE LOG

3 eggs

125 g (4 oz) caster sugar

125 g (4 oz) flour

1 tablespoon hot water

4 tablespoons apricot jam

100 g (3½ oz) butter, softened

220 g (7 oz) icing sugar

2 to 3 tablespoons warm milk

2 tablespoons cocoa

50 g (2 oz) chocolate, melted

Preheat the oven to 220°C (425°F).

Grease and line a 33 x 23 cm (13 x 9 in) swiss roll tin with greaseproof paper.

Place eggs and sugar in a large basin and whisk over a pan of hot water until light and creamy. Remove from heat and whisk until cool. Alternatively, beat eggs and sugar with an electric mixer until light and creamy.

Sift flour and gently fold half of it into mixture, using a metal spoon. Fold in rest of flour and stir in hot water.

Spread mixture in swiss roll tin and bake for 7 to 9 minutes until cooked and golden brown.

Meanwhile, lay a sheet of greaseproof paper (which is slightly larger than the swiss roll tin) on a damp tea towel, and sprinkle it with caster sugar. Warm apricot jam.

As soon as cake is cooked, turn it out onto the paper and peel off lining paper. Trim edges and spread whole surface with warmed jam. Roll sponge up widthways with the aid of the sugared paper, finishing with the end underneath.

Cut a diagonal slice from 1 end of roll, and place this on top of roll to form a 'knob'. Place cake on cake board or serving dish.

Cream butter until pale and fluffy. Beat in sugar a little at a time. Add sufficient milk to soften mixture.

Mix butter cream with cocoa and spread evenly over top, sides and ends of cake to completely cover it. Run a fork along top and sides to make horizontal grooves.

Place a little melted chocolate in a piping bag and pipe 3 or 4 concentric circles on the 'knob' and ends of the log to resemble rings on a tree trunk.

SERVES 6

Chocolate Chestnut Cake

Sauces and Toppings

QUICK RICH CHOCOLATE SAUCE

1½ tablespoons cocoa powder
170 g (6 oz) brown sugar
20 g (½ oz) butter
pinch salt
1 cup (250 ml/8 fl oz) cream

Boil all ingredients together for a few minutes. Serve immediately over pancakes, ice cream, fresh or stewed fruit or sponge pudding.

MAKES 2 CUPS (500 ML/16 FL OZ)

CHOCOLATE MINT SAUCE

12 chocolate peppermint creams
½ cup (125 ml/4 fl oz) cream

Put peppermint creams in a small bowl over a saucepan of boiling water. Allow chocolates to melt. Stir and slowly add cream. Serve warm or cold over ice cream or fruit.

SERVES 4

BASIC CHOCOLATE SAUCE

This simple, rich, smooth chocolate sauce can be used with freshly baked brioches or with hot puddings, fruit or ices.

180 g (6 oz) dark or cooking chocolate
125 g (4 oz) sugar
2½ cups (625 ml/21 fl oz) water

Cut chocolate into small pieces and melt in a bowl over a pan of hot water. Heat sugar and water in a saucepan, stirring continually until sugar dissolves. Boil syrup gently for 5 minutes. Carefully stir sugar syrup into chocolate. Return mixture to saucepan and, stirring continually, bring it to a simmer. Let it simmer for 7 to 10 minutes or until sauce thickly coats the back of a wooden spoon.

MAKES 2½ CUPS (625 ML/21 FL OZ)

CREAMY CHOCOLATE SAUCE

50 g (2 oz) drinking chocolate powder
1 cup (250 ml/8 fl oz) evaporated milk
1 tablespoon golden syrup
½ teaspoon vanilla essence
2 teaspoons butter

In a saucepan, combine drinking chocolate with evaporated milk and syrup. Bring mixture to the boil, over medium heat, stirring constantly. Simmer for 5 minutes. Remove from heat, add vanilla and butter. Serve hot.

MAKES 1¼ CUPS (310 ML/10 FL OZ)

CHOCOLATE GLACE ICING

200 g (6½ oz) icing sugar
1 tablespoon cocoa powder
1 teaspoon butter
1 tablespoon boiling water

Sift icing sugar and cocoa powder into a small heatproof bowl. Melt butter in boiling water then add to icing sugar mixture, stirring well to make a smooth paste. Place bowl over a saucepan of boiling water and stir mixture for 1 minute. Pour icing over your cake and smooth the surface with a spatula or knife dipped in hot water.

Note: To make plain glacé icing, omit the cocoa powder and butter. To make coffee glacé icing, add 1 tablespoon instant coffee instead powder of cocoa powder.

MAKES ENOUGH TO COVER A 20 CM (8 IN) CAKE

CHOCOLATE BUTTER ICING

250 g (8 oz) icing sugar
1 tablespoon cocoa powder
125 g (4 oz) butter
1 tablespoon sherry
few drops vanilla essence

Sift icing sugar and cocoa powder together. Beat butter until light and creamy. Gradually beat in half the icing sugar. Beat in sherry alternately with remaining icing sugar. Stir in vanilla essence.

MAKES ENOUGH TO FILL OR TOP A 20 CM (8 IN) CAKE

CARAQUE

50 g (2 oz) dark chocolate
knob of butter

Melt chocolate and butter over a double boiler. Allow to cool a little, then pour onto a hard flat surface, such as marble or the back of a metal baking dish or tray. Spread out quickly with a spatula. When chocolate is firm but not completely hard, scrape the surface with a heavy kitchen knife or a spatula warmed in hot water. Put the blade at a 45° angle to the table and push. The chocolate will form long cylindrical curls which will break very easily, so treat them with care. Avoid touching caraque if possible as the warmth of your hands will melt the chocolate very quickly.

Basic Chocolate Sauce

Copper pot from The Bay Tree

Desserts, Puddings and Ices

For the times when you feel like making something really special — from a cool, smooth, slide-down-your-throat summer dessert to a rich, hot winter warmer. Plus some hot drinks for cold nights made in minutes in your microwave.

Cakerstand, duck bowl, wire rack and cake slice from The Bay Tree, plates from Lifestyle Imports, fabric background 'South Pacific Greenbriar stripe 505 blush' from South Pacific Fabrics, glass jug from Kitchen Kapers

Coffee Cups

COFFEE CUPS

2½ cups (625 ml/21 fl oz) milk
60 g (2 oz) semolina
1 tablespoon instant coffee
110 g (3½ oz) caster sugar

SAUCE

45 g (1½ oz) brown sugar
4 tablespoons cocoa powder
⅔ cup (170 ml/6 fl oz) milk

Warm milk in a pan then sprinkle in semolina, coffee and sugar. Bring to the boil, stirring continuously. Cook, stirring, for a few more minutes, until semolina thickens.

Divide mixture between four 150 ml (5 fl oz) moulds that have been rinsed in cold water. Leave to cool and set.

To Prepare Sauce: Place all sauce ingredients in a pan. Stir over low heat to dissolve sugar and then boil for a few minutes stirring continually until sauce becomes smooth and thick. Serve hot or cold, over turned-out moulds.

Note: If you don't have suitable moulds, cups will do instead. A delicious way of jazzing up this pudding is to stir 1 tablespoon of Tia Maria, Crème de Cacao or brandy into the sauce before pouring it over the moulds.

Pictured on previous pages: Flourless Chocolate Berry Cake (page 31) and Poire William Chocolate Tart (page 46)

CREPES TIA MARIA

125 g (4 oz) flour
1 tablespoon caster sugar
pinch of salt
2 eggs
2 egg yolks
1¼ cups (310 ml/10 fl oz) milk
1 tablespoon melted butter
2 tablespoons Tia Maria
extra butter
extra Tia Maria

Blend everything except extra butter and extra Tia Maria until mixture is smooth. Cover and leave to stand for 1 hour.

Pour a little mixture into a lightly-greased crêpe pan and cook over a medium heat on both sides until golden. Mixture will make 14 to 16 small crêpes.

To Prepare the Crêpes: Fold each crêpe in four to make a triangle. Heat a little butter and Tia Maria in a frypan, add some folded crêpes and heat gently for a few minutes. Keep crêpes warm until served. Serve with Quick Rich Chocolate Sauce (see recipe, page 24).

Note: Crêpes may be made in advance and stored, covered, in the refrigerator.

SERVES 4 TO 6

STACKING CREPES/PANCAKES

Place sheets of greaseproof paper between the crêpes when they are cooked. This will prevent them sticking together.

Crêpes Tia Maria

Beat the batter until it is bubbly.

Tilt the pan to thinly coat the pan with batter.

Loosen the edges with a palette knife.

Chocolate Walnut Pancakes

CHOCOLATE WALNUT PANCAKES

WALNUT FILLING

- 60 g (2 oz) sultanas
- 1 to 2 tablespoons rum
- 80 g (2½ oz) butter, at room temperature
- 125 g (4 oz) walnuts, very finely chopped
- 165 g (5½ oz) caster sugar
- few drops vanilla essence
- 3 tablespoons cream

CHOCOLATE SAUCE

- 100 g (3½ oz) dark or cooking chocolate
- 2 teaspoons cornflour
- 1 cup (250 ml/8 fl oz) milk
- 2 teaspoons caster sugar
- 3 tablespoons cream
- ½ teaspoon cinnamon

BASIC PANCAKE BATTER

- 100 g (3½ oz) flour
- ½ teaspoon salt
- 1 egg
- 1¼ cups (310 ml/10 fl oz) milk
- oil for frying

To Make the Filling: Soak sultanas in rum for 15 minutes. Soften butter and blend in walnuts, sugar, vanilla and cream. Mix well, then add rum and fruit.

To Make the Sauce: Break chocolate into a small pan and add 3 tablespoons cold water. Stir over gentle heat until melted and smooth. Blend cornflour with a little milk and stir this into chocolate with sugar and remaining milk. Gradually bring to the boil and simmer for 5 minutes, stirring. Remove from heat and stir in cream and cinnamon.

To Make the Pancakes: Sieve flour and salt into a bowl. Add egg and ⅔ cup (160 ml/5 fl oz) milk and beat thoroughly until smooth. Mix in remaining milk and beat until bubbly.

Heat a 15 cm (6 in) frying pan over a fairly high heat. Brush with a little oil.

Pour in a little batter, tilting pan to thinly coat base. Cook quickly, shaking pan and loosening edge of pancake with a palette knife until underside is golden brown. Toss pancake and cook other side.

Slide cooked pancake onto a plate and keep it warm, covered with a second plate. Repeat with remaining batter, to make 8 to 10 pancakes.

Put a little walnut filling onto each cooked pancake, roll up pancakes and transfer to a heated serving dish. Cover and keep warm.

Gently reheat chocolate sauce and pour it over pancakes. Serve immediately.

SERVES 4

FLOURLESS CHOCOLATE BERRY CAKE

500 g (16 oz) dark or cooking chocolate, broken into small pieces

430 g (13½ oz) unsalted butter, cubed

280g (9 oz) sugar

10 eggs, separated

¼ cup (60 ml/2 fl oz) framboise liqueur

2 teaspoons vanilla essence

SAUCE

500g (16 oz) fresh or frozen berries (raspberries, blackberries, loganberries etc)

¼ cup (60 ml/2 fl oz) framboise liqueur

60 g (2 oz) vanilla sugar

icing sugar, to serve

extra fresh berries, for decoration

Preheat the oven to 130°C (275°F).

Melt chocolate and butter in a large bowl over a saucepan of simmering water. Add 1 cup sugar, stirring until dissolved, about 3 minutes.

Beat egg yolks in a large bowl until blended, then stir in 1 cup chocolate mixture. Return to remaining chocolate mixture, and cook, stirring constantly, until slightly thickened, about 4 minutes. Do not boil. Remove from heat and stir in framboise and vanilla.

Whisk egg whites until just beginning to stiffen, then, while beating, gradually, add remaining sugar. Beat until mixture is stiff and glossy. Gently fold into chocolate mixture.

Butter and base-line two 23 cm (9 in) springform cake tins. Lightly dust with caster sugar. Pour mixture into tins, bake in centre of oven for 2 hours, or until firm. Cool in tin, remove, wrap in foil and refrigerate until chilled. Freeze one cake for another time.

To Make the Sauce: Blend berries, liqueur, sugar and vanilla sugar. Strain through a coarse sieve, if desired, or leave as is. Dust cake liberally with icing sugar and serve thin wedges in a pool of sauce, decorated with fresh berries. Pass whipped cream around separately, if desired.

SERVES 12 TO 14

Flourless Chocolate Berry Cake

CHOCOLATE ORANGE CHEESECAKE

250 g (8 oz) wheatmeal biscuits

100 g (3½ oz) butter

pinch cinnamon

¼ cup (60 ml/2 fl oz) milk

90 g (3 oz) dark or cooking chocolate

250 g (8 oz) cream cheese

2 tablespoons water

1 tablespoon powdered gelatine

juice and grated rind 1 orange

⅔ cup (170 ml/6 fl oz) whipped cream

caramelised orange rind (see recipe, page 42)

To Make the Base: Crush wheatmeal biscuits. Melt butter and blend with crushed biscuits and cinnamon.

Grease bottom and sides of a loose-bottomed 20 cm (8 in) cake tin with butter. Spread biscuit mixture over base of tin. Refrigerate while preparing filling.

To Make the Filling: Place milk and chocolate in saucepan and heat gently, stirring until chocolate melts.

Chocolate Orange Cheesecake

Mix well with cream cheese.

Heat water and dissolve gelatine in it. Reheat until you have a clear, jelly-like substance. Stir gelatine into cream cheese with orange rind and juice. Fold in whipped cream, and then pour mixture into tin.

Chill in refrigerator for 3 hours until set and firm. Remove cheesecake from tin and place on a serving plate. Decorate top with caramelised orange rind.

SERVES 6 TO 8

COOLING CHOCOLATE

Cool chocolate at room temperature. This helps to maintain the gloss.

CHOCOLATE COINTREAU MOUSSE

250 g (8 oz) dark or cooking chocolate

3 tablespoons strong black coffee

20 g (½ oz) butter

1 tablespoon Cointreau

3 large eggs, separated

1 cup (250 ml/8 fl oz) whipped cream, for decoration

caraque (see recipe, page 24)

Break chocolate bar into small pieces. Place chocolate and black coffee in a small bowl standing over a pan of hot water over gentle heat. Stir continuously until chocolate melts and becomes creamy. Cook gently for 2 to 3 minutes.

Remove bowl and stir in butter and Cointreau until butter dissolves. Cool slightly before beating in egg yolks.

Whisk egg whites until stiff and fold them into chocolate mixture. Spoon into glasses or individual dishes and chill in refrigerator until set (about 1 hour). Serve decorated with a swirl of whipped cream and caraque (see recipe, page 24).

This mousse is very rich and a little goes a long way. It looks attractive served in small china pots and can then be stretched to serve 6 people.

SERVES 4

Chocolate Cointreau Mousse

CHOCOLATE CHARLOTTE

1 plain sponge cake

2 tablespoons rum

2 eggs, separated

55 g (2 oz) caster sugar

1¼ cups (310 ml/10 fl oz) milk

30 g (1 oz) dark or cooking chocolate, grated

1½ tablespoons gelatine

⅔ cup (170 ml/6 fl oz) thickened cream, whipped

Cut a 1 cm (½ in) layer off flat base of sponge cake. Place top half upside-down in a round dish or pudding bowl. Sprinkle with rum.

Cream egg yolks with sugar until pale and fluffy.

Bring milk to the boil in a thick-bottomed pan. Stir in chocolate until melted. Pour milk into egg mixture, stirring well.

Clean saucepan and return mixture to it, cooking over low heat and stirring all the time until mixture coats the back of a spoon. Do not boil. Remove from heat and add gelatine, stirring until it is dissolved. Leave to cool, stirring from time to time until almost set.

In a separate bowl, beat cream. Fold it into mixture. Beat egg whites until stiff, and fold them into chocolate mixture.

Pour mixture over rum-flavoured sponge and top with remaining slice of sponge. Chill and serve with custard or whipped cream.

Note: This recipe can be varied by substituting a different liqueur, such as Grand Marnier, for the rum, or using a chocolate- or coffee-flavoured sponge cake. The top of the cake can be decorated with whipped cream or dusted with icing sugar.

SERVES 4 TO 6

GELATO PRONTO

This is an Italian favourite with layers of ice cream, chocolate sauce and cream.

30 g (1 oz) dark or cooking chocolate

30 g (1 oz) milk chocolate or coffee-flavoured chocolate

2 tablespoons custard powder

110 g (3½ oz) caster sugar

5 to 6 tablespoons cocoa powder

2½ cups (625 ml/21 fl oz) milk

1 teaspoon vanilla essence

1½ cups (375 ml/12 fl oz) thickened cream

120 g (4 oz) whole blanched almonds

TOPPING

⅔ cup (170 ml/6 fl oz) cream

1 tablespoon caster sugar

few drops vanilla essence

60 g (2 oz) dark or cooking chocolate

Grate dark chocolate into one mixing bowl, and milk or coffee-flavoured chocolate into another.

Dissolve custard powder, sugar and cocoa in a quarter of the milk. Heat rest of milk in a pan. Stir in custard mixture and cook for 3 minutes, beating constantly. Add vanilla.

Remove from heat and divide custard between the 2 mixing bowls containing grated chocolate. Stir custard into each one until chocolate is melted.

Allow custard mixtures to cool, beating from time to time to prevent a skin forming.

When custards are almost cold, beat cream until thick. Beat half the cream into each custard. Pour mixtures into 2 freezer trays. Freeze until they start to form ice but are still soft. Transfer to separate bowls and beat thoroughly. Freeze until firm.

To Make the Topping: Beat cream with sugar and vanilla. Melt chocolate in a bowl over hot water.

When ready to serve, divide scoops of ice cream among 6 ice cream glasses, mixing the 2 flavours. Arrange almonds among the ice cream balls, reserving 6 for garnish.

Top each glass with whipped cream, pour melted chocolate over and garnish with a single almond. Serve immediately.

SERVES 6

BEATING ICES

Beating ice creams halfway through the freezing process breaks up the ice crystals leaving a smoother, creamier dessert. Timing here is important. If you beat it too early it will liquidise.

CHOCOLATE BANANA COUPES

3 ripe bananas

2 tablespoons rum

2½ cups (625 ml/21 fl oz) thickened cream

185 g (6 oz) dark or cooking chocolate, finely grated

4 scoops vanilla or coffee ice cream

grated chocolate to garnish

Slice bananas very thinly and sprinkle with rum.

Whip cream until thick. Mix ¼ of cream with chocolate and reserve this for decoration. Add bananas and rum to remaining cream, and spoon mixture into 4 individual serving dishes.

Just before serving, top each dish with a scoop of ice cream. Pipe chocolate cream around ice cream and sprinkle grated chocolate over.

SERVES 4

MELTING CHOCOLATE

Melt chocolate slowly without stirring, although some cooks advocate working it with a palette knife if it is to be used for coating cakes or making chocolate cases, because that helps to keep the gloss when it sets. The chocolate should be no more than lukewarm.

CHOCOLATE RUM SOUFFLE

1¾ cups (450 ml/14½ fl oz) milk

4 tablespoons cocoa powder

75 g (2½ oz) caster sugar

3 large eggs, separated

2 teaspoons rum

⅔ cup (170 ml/6 fl oz) cream

⅓ cup (85 ml/3 fl oz) warm water

1½ tablespoons powdered gelatine

60 g (2 oz) chocolate, made into curls or caraque (see recipe, page 24)

Fold a doubled sheet of greaseproof paper around a 2 cup (500ml/ 16 fl oz) soufflé dish, so that paper reaches at least 5 cm (2 in) above rim, and tie it in place with string. Lightly grease inside of dish and paper.

Blend milk and cocoa in a pan and bring them to the boil, stirring. In a bowl, cream together sugar, egg yolks and rum. Gradually pour in chocolate milk, still stirring. Return mixture to pan and heat gently, without boiling, stirring constantly, until it thickens. Allow to cool a little.

Beat cream until thick and stir it into custard. Dissolve gelatine in water and add to half-cooled custard. Leave custard in a cool place until on the point of setting.

In a clean bowl, beat egg whites until stiff. Fold into chocolate custard and pour mixture into prepared soufflé dish. Leave in a cool place or in refrigerator until set.

Undo string and remove paper by holding a sharp knife alongside soufflé dish and peeling paper carefully away. Sprinkle edge of soufflé with chocolate curls or caraque. Serve at once.

Note: Vary this recipe by adding a liqueur of your choice instead of rum.

SERVES 6

CHOCOLATE ORANGE TRIFLE

1 chocolate swiss roll

2 tablespoons Grand Marnier

2 oranges

2½ cups (625 ml/21 fl oz) chocolate custard

⅔ cup (170 ml/6 fl oz) whipped cream

6 glacé cherries, halved

50 g (2 oz) grated chocolate

Cut swiss roll into slices about 2 cm (¾ in) thick and use them to line a glass dish as evenly as possible. Sprinkle with Grand Marnier.

Finely grate rind of one orange and reserve. Peel both oranges, remove pith and cut oranges in thin slices across segments, removing pips. Cut slices in half and arrange over cake.

Pour custard over orange and cake slices and chill until set. Beat cream until thick then fold in grated orange rind. Decorate top of trifle with whipped cream, glacé cherries and grated chocolate. Serve cold.

SERVES 6

GRATING ORANGE RIND

When grating orange rind, ensure that there is no white pith — this is very bitter.

SHERRY MOCHA DESSERT

150 g (5 oz) butter
150 g (5 oz) caster sugar
50 g (2 oz) cocoa powder, sifted
125 g (4 oz) mixed nuts, chopped
2 eggs
1 tablespoon sherry
1 tablespoon cream
¾ cup (185 ml/6 fl oz) strong black coffee
2 double 20 cm (8 in) trifle sponges or thick sponge slices

DECORATION

250 g (8 oz) soft butter
465 g (15 oz) icing sugar
1 tablespoon cocoa powder
¼ cup (60 ml/2 fl oz) cream
few drops vanilla essence
30 g (1 oz) chocolate, melted
12 roasted hazelnuts

Line the length and sides of a greased 1 kg (2 lb) loaf tin with greaseproof paper, and grease paper well.

Cream butter and sugar until light and fluffy. Beat in sifted cocoa, chopped nuts and eggs.

In a clean bowl, mix sherry and cream with strong coffee. Trim sponges to fit tin. Brush two sponges with coffee mixture and place them side by side on base of tin. Spread cocoa butter mixture on top of coffee-soaked sponge. Brush remaining sponges with coffee and press them level on top. Cover and chill overnight.

To Make the Decoration: Cream together butter, icing sugar, cocoa, cream and vanilla essence, adding a little more cream if necessary to give a spreading consistency. Dip base of the loaf tin in warm water and turn dessert out onto a serving plate. Cut ends to neaten.

Fill a piping bag fitted with a star nozzle with butter cream and pipe over top and sides of cake. Decorate with melted chocolate and arrange the hazelnuts on top. Serve chilled.

SERVES 8

Sherry Mocha Dessert

CHOCOLATE CASTLES WITH FUDGY SAUCE

75 g (2½ oz) margarine
75 g (2½ oz) caster sugar
1 egg
½ teaspoon vanilla essence
100 g (3½ oz) self-raising flour
3 tablespoons cocoa powder
milk to mix

Fudgy Sauce

120 g (4 oz) chocolate caramel bars
¼ cup (60 ml/2 fl oz) water

Preheat the oven to 180°C (350°F).

Lightly grease 4 individual 1 cup (250 ml/8 fl oz) custard cups or soufflé dishes and line bases with greaseproof paper.

Beat margarine and sugar together until pale and fluffy, then beat in egg and vanilla essence. Sift flour and cocoa powder together and fold into creamed mixture with a little milk, to give a soft dropping consistency.

Transfer mixture to prepared custard cups and bake for about 25 minutes, until well risen and firm to touch.

Just before puddings are cooked, make a fudgy sauce; cut up chocolate caramel bars and place pieces in a pan with water. Stir over gentle heat until bars melt.

Turn out cooked puddings onto individual serving dishes and pour sauce over them. Serve hot.

SERVES 4

CHOCOLATE CUSTARD

To make chocolate custard, melt the chocolate in the milk, then proceed as usual.

CHOCOLATE MARBLE PUDDING

150 g (5 oz) self-raising flour
pinch salt
100 g (3½ oz) butter
100 g (3½ oz) caster sugar
2 beaten eggs
a little milk
grated rind 1 lemon
few drops vanilla essence
2 tablespoons cocoa powder

Sift together flour and salt. Cream butter and sugar in a mixing bowl, food processor or blender until light and fluffy.

Add beaten eggs gradually, beating all the time, then fold in sifted flour, ½ at a time. Stir in a little milk so mixture is not too stiff.

Divide mixture between 2 bowls and add lemon rind and vanilla essence to one and cocoa to the other.

Grease a 1 litre (35 fl oz) pudding basin and add lemon and chocolate mixtures alternately, a spoonful at a time.

Cover securely with greased greaseproof paper or aluminium foil, tie with string and steam for 1½ to 2 hours. Serve this pudding very hot with chocolate sauce (see recipes page 24).

Note: You can use other flavourings and colourings to make a marble pudding. Try adding coffee essence, grated orange rind and juice or even cochineal to achieve different effects and flavours. Always add the different coloured mixtures in spoonfuls to get an attractive marbled effect.

SERVES 6

Divide the pudding mixture between 2 bowls, adding lemon to one and cocoa to the other.

Add the mixtures alternately to the pudding basin.

Cover the basin securely with aluminium foil.

PETITS POTS AU CHOCOLAT

100 g (3½ oz) dark or cooking chocolate

2½ cups (625 ml/21 fl oz) milk

2 eggs

2 egg yolks

2 tablespoons caster sugar

2 teaspoons rum

½ cup (125 ml/4 fl oz) thickened cream, whipped

Preheat the oven to 170°C (325°F).

Grate one square of chocolate for decoration. Combine remaining chocolate and milk in a pan and heat to melt chocolate.

Beat eggs, egg yolks and sugar together until light, then pour in hot but not boiling milk, stirring all the time. Stir in rum, then strain mixture into 6 individual ovenproof dishes.

Stand dishes in a baking dish, half fill it with hot water, bake for 40 to 60 minutes or until custards are lightly set.

Serve hot or cold, and decorate with whipped cream and grated chocolate.

SERVES 6

CHOCOLATE CREAM

To melt chocolate in fresh cream, first heat the cream in a heavy-based saucepan on a low heat. Add pieces of chocolate and stir until just melted. Allow to cool then beat by hand or with an electric beater. Use immediately (before it hardens) to cover cakes or desserts.

MARASCHINO CHARLOTTE

4 eggs, separated

110 g (3½ oz) caster sugar

2½ cups (625 ml/21 fl oz) milk

60 g (2 oz) dark or cooking chocolate, chopped

2 tablespoons powdered gelatine

1¼ cups (315 ml/10 fl oz) thickened cream

12 sponge fingers

2 tablespoons maraschino liqueur

6 glacé cherries

Beat egg yolks with sugar until pale and fluffy. Heat milk and stir into egg mixture. Stir in chopped chocolate until melted. Cook over low heat until the mixture coats a spoon. Do not boil. Dissolve gelatine in a tablespoon of hot water and stir into mixture. Leave it to cool.

Beat ¾ cup (180 ml/6 fl oz) cream until stiff and fold into chocolate mixture.

Beat egg whites until stiff and fold into mixture.

Pour a little chocolate mixture into the bottom of a charlotte mould. Sprinkle sponge fingers with maraschino liqueur and arrange around the edge of the mould.

Pour in remaining chocolate mixture and leave mould in a cool place until set. Beat remaining cream until stiff. Turn mould out onto a serving dish and decorate with piped cream and glacé cherries. Serve at once.

SERVES 6

MARRON MONT BLANC

2 x 15 cm (6 in) sandwich sponges

6 tablespoons rum

90 g (3 oz) dark or cooking chocolate

440 g (14 oz) canned sweetened chestnut purée

⅔ cup (170 ml/6 fl oz) thickened cream

Sprinkle sponges with 4 tablespoons rum.

Melt chocolate in a bowl over a pan of hot water and stir into chestnut purée with remaining rum.

Whip cream until just thick and fold half into chestnut mixture.

Make a sandwich of the two sponges with some chestnut mixture and transfer to a serving plate. Pipe or spread remaining chestnut mixture around and on top of sponge cakes.

Put remaining cream in a piping bag fitted with a small star nozzle. Decorate top of dessert with a large swirl of cream and pipe small rosettes around the base.

SERVES 6 TO 8

PEARS HELENE

2½ cups (625 ml/21 fl oz) water
220 g (7 oz) caster sugar
1 vanilla pod, split
4 pears, peeled
375 ml (12 fl oz) ice cream

PRALINE

110 g (3½ oz) caster sugar
125 g (4 oz) mixed nuts, chopped
oil for greasing

CHOCOLATE SAUCE

250 g (8 oz) dark or cooking chocolate
2 cups (500 ml/16 fl oz) water
1 tablespoon sugar
few drops vanilla essence
3 tablespoons cream
2 teaspoons butter

To Prepare the Syrup: Combine water and sugar in a saucepan. Bring gradually to the boil, stirring continually, until sugar dissolves. Boil syrup for 1 minute and remove from heat. Immediately add vanilla pod. Cover and let syrup slowly cool so it becomes impregnated with vanilla flavour.

While syrup cools, make praline. Place sugar and 1 tablespoon of water in a heavy-based saucepan. Slowly heat sugar until it begins to caramelise or turn golden. This should happen at 149°C (300°F).

Stir in nuts and turn praline mixture onto a lightly-oiled metal tray or shallow cake tin. Allow to cool. When set, break up and crush into small pieces with a rolling pin.

Preheat the oven to 190°C (375°F).

Place pears in a shallow ovenproof dish. Remove vanilla pod (wash and dry it for re-use) and pour syrup over pears. Poach pears in oven for 35 minutes, basting and turning frequently to prevent them browning and drying out. Cover and cool in the syrup.

To Prepare the Sauce: Dissolve chocolate in water over a gentle heat. Stir in sugar and vanilla essence and cook sauce over a low heat for 20 to 25 minutes. Stir in cream and butter and keep sauce warm.

Just before serving, spread ice cream over the bottom of a shallow serving dish. Drain pears and arrange them on top. Spoon some sauce and crushed praline over pears and serve with a bowl of hot chocolate sauce.

SERVES 4

BANANA BOATS

300 ml (10 fl oz) vanilla ice cream
4 peeled bananas
2 tablespoons chopped nuts

CHOCOLATE SAUCE

250 g (8 oz) dark or cooking chocolate
2 cups (500 ml/16 fl oz) water
1 tablespoon sugar
few drops vanilla essence
3 tablespoons cream
7½ g (¼ oz) butter

Prepare chocolate sauce following instructions in Pears Hélène recipe (above). Allow sauce to cool.

Place 2 scoops of ice cream in each of 4 banana split dishes. Place a banana on top and pour chocolate sauce over. Sprinkle each serving with chopped nuts and serve immediately.

SERVES 4

CHOCOLATE ICE CREAM

5 egg yolks
155 g (5 oz) caster sugar
2 cups (500 ml/16 fl oz) milk
5 to 6 tablespoons cocoa powder

Whisk egg yolks and sugar until mixture is thick and creamy.

Heat milk in a pan, and when it is almost boiling, whisk in cocoa powder. Add hot chocolate milk gradually to eggs and sugar, stirring continually to mix well.

Pour mixture into a clean pan, and stir over low heat with a wooden spoon until mixture coats the back of a spoon. Transfer mixture to an ice cream churn and churn until frozen, or pour into a freezer tray and freeze, stirring from time to time.

Press frozen ice cream into an ice cream mould and return to freezer. To serve, dip mould in hot water for a few seconds and invert ice cream onto a chilled plate.

SERVES 6

ICE MOUNTAIN

250 g (8 oz) dark or cooking chocolate

2 tablespoons sugar

2 to 3 tablespoons lime juice cordial

250 g (8 oz) plain sponge cake

2 eggs, separated

1 cup (250 ml/8 fl oz) thickened cream

Reserve 2 squares of chocolate and melt rest with sugar and lime juice in a basin over a pan of hot water.

Meanwhile, slice sponge cake thinly and use some slices to line a 1.5 litre (52 fl oz) pudding basin. Fill in gaps with pieces of cake cut to fit.

When chocolate has melted, leave it to cool slightly and then beat in egg yolks. Whisk egg whites until stiff. In a separate bowl, whisk half the cream until firm peaks form. Blend chocolate with cream then fold in whisked egg whites.

Spoon some chocolate mixture into basin so that sponge on the bottom is well covered. Arrange a layer of sponge on top, again filling gaps, and coat it with a little of the chocolate. Repeat process until all chocolate has been used up, and end with sponge.

Ice Mountain

Place a plate, same size as top of bowl, on top. Press it down with weights and leave pudding in refrigerator for a day.

Whip remaining cream. Ease a metal spatula down sides of bowl and turn pudding out onto a serving plate. Spread whipped cream over pudding. Grate reserved chocolate and sprinkle it over the top.

SERVES 6

Place the sponge in the bottom of the pan and the sponge fingers around the sides.

Stir the egg yolks and the instant coffee into the melted chocolate.

Pour the mixture into the prepared sponge case.

PARADISE RING

Paradise Ring

- *20 sponge fingers*
- *1 round sponge cake, 18 cm (7 in) in diameter*
- *400 g (13 oz) dark or cooking chocolate*
- *8 eggs, separated*
- *2 tablespoons instant coffee*
- *4 tablespoons powdered gelatine*
- *½ cup (125 ml/4 fl oz) hot water*
- *1 cup (250 ml/8 fl oz) thickened cream*
- *additional melted chocolate for decoration*

Lightly grease a 20 cm (8 in) round loose-bottomed cake tin. Trim sponge fingers to roughly the same size. Place sponge cake in centre of tin and pack sponge fingers in gap around edge, flat side against the cake.

Melt 300 g (10 oz) chocolate in a fairly large bowl over a pan of hot water. Stir in egg yolks and instant coffee. Dissolve gelatine in hot water and when quite clear, stir into chocolate mixture. Leave to cool slightly. Whisk egg whites until stiff and fold into chocolate mixture. Turn mixture into prepared tin and leave for several hours to set (see note).

Lightly whip cream until just stiff. Melt remaining chocolate. Spread the cream over chocolate mousse and drop in chocolate, swirling it with a skewer to give a marbled effect. Carefully push up base of tin and slide pudding onto a plate. Tie a ribbon around the sponge fingers to keep them in place. Dribble additional melted chocolate over tops of sponge fingers and pipe any remaining cream around base.

Note: Gelatine mixtures tend to toughen in the refrigerator so the ring is better left to set in some other cool place.

SERVES 8 TO 10

CHOCOLATE RUM FONDUE

250 g (8 oz) dark or cooking chocolate

½ cup (125 ml/4 fl oz) thickened cream

2 tablespoons rum

2 tablespoons orange juice

3 mandarins, segmented

2 apples, cored and sliced

2 bananas, sliced

250 g (8 oz) canned pineapple pieces, drained

½ lemon

Break chocolate into squares and melt with cream, rum and orange juice in a fondue dish or heatproof bowl over a pan of hot water. Keep warm.

Arrange pieces of fruit decoratively in a bowl with small wooden forks or cocktail sticks. Squeeze lemon over fruit to preserve its colour.

Invite guests to dip fruit of their choice into chocolate rum sauce. Alternatively, serve your fondue with sponge finger biscuits.

SERVES 6

CHOCOLATE DRINKS

To make a chocolate drink, chop 125 g (4 oz) of chocolate into 1 litre (35 fl oz) of milk and allow it to melt slowly over a low heat, stirring occasionally.

CHOCOLATE CHEESECAKE

BASE

170 g (6 oz) wheatmeal biscuits

40 g (1½ oz) butter

40 g (1½ oz) chocolate

FILLING

3 medium eggs

75 g (2½ oz) caster sugar

1 large orange

½ lemon

350 g (11½ oz) cottage cheese

1 tablespoon gelatine

⅔ cup (170 ml/6 fl oz) thickened cream

30 g (1 oz) chocolate, for decoration

To Make the Base: Crush biscuits finely. Melt butter and chocolate together over a gentle heat. Take off heat and stir in biscuits until evenly coated in chocolate.

Press mixture into base of an 18 cm (7 in) loose-bottomed cake tin. Chill until firm (5 hours minimum).

To Make the Filling: Separate eggs and place yolks in a basin with sugar. Whisk until thick and creamy. Grate rind of orange and lemon into egg mixture. Sieve cottage cheese into mixture.

Squeeze juice from orange and lemon into a small saucepan. Sprinkle gelatine over fruit juices. Allow to soften for 5 minutes. Place pan over very low heat and leave until liquid is clear, about 3 minutes. Cool slightly.

Meanwhile, beat egg and cheese mixture in a bowl until smooth. Pour in cooled, dissolved gelatine and fruit juice in a thin stream, stirring all the time. Whip cream until it just holds its shape. Fold into mixture.

Whisk egg whites until stiff. Fold into cheesecake mixture using a metal spoon. Spoon filling over chocolate biscuit-crumb base. Refrigerate for several hours or overnight if preferred.

When firm, unmould onto a serving plate. Melt chocolate in a basin over hot water, and put in a greaseproof piping bag. Drizzle it in a decorative pattern over cheesecake. Allow to set before serving.

SERVES 8

CARAMELISED ORANGE RIND

2 oranges, peeled in strips

60 g (2 oz) sugar

¼ cup (60 ml/2 fl oz) water

2 tablespoons Grand Marnier or Cointreau

Cut orange peel into julienne strips. Place in a saucepan and cover with cold water. Slowly bring to the boil then cover pan. Simmer for 10 minutes. Drain.

Place sugar in a pan with water. Stir over a low heat until sugar dissolves. Bring to the boil and cook fairly briskly until syrup becomes tacky and thickish. Remove from heat. Cool slightly.

Stir in Grand Marnier or Cointreau. Add peel to syrup. Cook gently until peel begins to look transparent. Remove with a slotted spoon. Cool, then use peel for decoration.

WHISKY PRUNE CHOCOLATE CAKE

110 g (3½ oz) sliced pitted prunes

½ cup (125 ml/4 fl oz) whisky

420 g (13 oz) dark or cooking chocolate

250 g (8 oz) unsalted butter

6 eggs, separated

300 g (10 oz) caster sugar

160 g (5 oz) plain flour

250 g (8 oz) blanched almonds, finely ground

pinch salt

Icing

250 g (8 oz) dark or cooking chocolate

1 cup (250 ml/8 fl oz) thick cream

Preheat the oven to 180°C (350°F).

Soak prunes in whisky for several hours or overnight. Melt chocolate and ¼ cup (60 ml/2 fl oz) of water in a large bowl over a saucepan of simmering water. Add butter gradually, stirring after each addition until mixture is smooth. Remove from heat and cool slightly.

Beat egg yolks with sugar until thick and pale. Stir into chocolate. Mix in flour and almonds, then prunes and whisky, until combined.

Beat egg whites with salt until stiff but not dry. Carefully fold egg whites, in three batches, into chocolate mixture. Pour into a buttered, base-lined and lightly-floured 25 to 30 cm (10 to 12 in) cake tin. Bake for 45 minutes, or until cake is shrinking from sides of pan and still slightly moist in the centre. Cool, then refrigerate in tin until firm. Turn onto a wire rack.

To Make the Icing: Melt chocolate with cream, stirring until smooth. Cool a little, then pour over cold cake, spreading around sides also. Allow to set, then carefully transfer cake to a serving plate. Refrigerate until 30 minutes before required.

Serve with blueberries and cream if desired.

SERVES 15 TO 20

MELTED CHOCOLATE

Chop or break chocolate into small pieces before melting so it melts quickly and evenly. Do not stir chocolate while it melts. Test that chocolate is melted by dipping the point of a knife into the centre.

CHOCOLATE ALMOND STEAMED PUDDING

125 g (4 oz) unsalted butter

125 g (4 oz) icing sugar

125 g (4 oz) dark or cooking chocolate, grated

125 g (4 oz) blanched almonds, ground

6 eggs, separated

butter and caster sugar for basin

Cream butter and icing sugar until light and fluffy. Mix in chocolate, almonds and egg yolks, beating until soft and light. Whisk egg whites until stiff peaks form, then gently fold into chocolate mixture.

Butter inside of a 1.2 litre (40 fl oz) pudding basin, then sprinkle lightly with caster sugar. Spoon prepared mixture into basin, cover with baking paper and then foil, and tie with string. Place basin in a large pot, pour in hot water to come halfway up sides of basin, cover pot and simmer over moderate heat for 1 hour. Remove basin from pot, invert onto a serving plate and remove pudding. Serve hot with cream.

SERVES 6

TIRAMISU

2 egg yolks

3 tablespoons vanilla sugar

375 g (12 oz) mascarpone

1 cup (250 ml/8 fl oz) strong black coffee, cold

2 tablespoons Kahlua

18 Savoiardi or ladyfinger biscuits

2 to 3 tablespoons cocoa

Mix egg yolks and sugar with a wooden spoon until creamy. Fold in mascarpone until smooth. Combine coffee and liqueur. Dip biscuits for 1 to 2 seconds in liquid, allowing them to absorb just enough to remain firm but not fall apart. Arrange layers of biscuits, then mascarpone mixture, in 8 individual 1 cup (250 ml/8 fl oz) soufflé dishes, finishing with a mascarpone layer. Dust with cocoa and refrigerate until chilled and set.

SERVES 8

GRATING CITRUS FRUIT

When grating orange rind, ensure that there is no white pith — this is very bitter.

BANANA CREAM

100 g (3½ oz) dark or cooking chocolate

1¼ cups (310 ml/10 fl oz) thickened cream

2 large ripe bananas

Reserve 2 squares of chocolate and melt remainder in a bowl over a pan of hot water. Remove from heat and allow melted chocolate to cool slightly.

Whisk cream until it forms stiff peaks, being careful not to over-whip.

Mash bananas and fold them with chocolate into cream. Divide banana cream between 4 glasses and grate a little reserved chocolate over the top of each. Chill and serve.

SERVES 4

BANANAS

Once peeled, bananas should be used promptly or they will discolour. Sprinkle with lemon juice if they are to be left for a while.

ORANGE AND CHOCOLATE SOUFFLE

40 g (1½ oz) cocoa powder

1¾ cups (450 ml/14½ fl oz) milk

3 large eggs, separated

finely grated rind and juice 1 orange

75 g (2½ oz) caster sugar

1 tablespoon powdered gelatine

1¼ cups (310 ml/10 fl oz) thickened cream

60 g (2 oz) dark or cooking chocolate, grated

Place a double band of greaseproof paper around a 4 cup (1 litre/1¾ pint) soufflé dish to come 5 cm (2 in) above rim, and tie it securely with string. Very lightly butter dish and paper.

Put cocoa and milk in a pan. Bring to the boil, stirring. Blend egg yolks with orange rind, juice and sugar and stir in chocolate milk. Return the mixture to pan and stir over gentle heat until custard thickens. Remove from heat.

Dissolve gelatine in 3 tablespoons hot water. Mix with custard, then cool over a bowl of ice until just beginning to set.

Whip half the cream until just thick. Whisk egg whites until stiff but not dry. Fold cream into custard, then fold in egg whites. Transfer mixture to a prepared soufflé dish. Leave to set completely.

Remove paper band from set soufflé. Whip remaining cream, spread a little around soufflé sides. Press grated chocolate on this. Pipe remaining cream in swirls around the top.

SERVES 6

Place a double band of greaseproof paper around the soufflé dish, and tie it securely.

Stir the egg mixture into the chocolate milk.

Fold the egg whites into the cool custard mixture.

Orange and Chocolate Soufflé

NEGRE EN CHEMISE

A classic chocolate soufflé from Vienna — served cold with lashings of cream and guaranteed not to let the cook down.

225 g (7 oz) cooking chocolate
½ teaspoon instant coffee
2 tablespoons Grand Marnier
6 large eggs, separated
175 g (6 oz) sugar
175 g (6 oz) softened butter
pinch of cream of tartar
⅔ cup (170 ml/6 fl oz) cream, for serving

CREAM TOPPING

⅔ cup (170 ml/6 fl oz) thickened cream
2 tablespoons sherry

Break chocolate into a bowl.

Dissolve coffee in 3 tablespoons hot water and add to chocolate. Add Grand Marnier.

Place bowl over a pan of hot water on very low heat. Stir until chocolate has melted. Set aside.

Beat egg yolks with sugar and butter until creamy. Stir into melted chocolate. Leave until mixture has cooled.

Whisk egg whites with cream of tartar until very stiff. Fold into chocolate mixture.

Butter a 7 cup (1.7 litre/55 fl oz) tall pudding bowl. Pour mixture in and make a slight hollow in centre with the back of a spoon. Cover top of mould tightly with foil tied with string.

Place bowl in a pan with water reaching halfway up the sides. Bring water to the boil, cover pan and leave to steam for 1½ hours. Top up with extra water during cooking if necessary. When soufflé is firm, remove from pan and leave to cool.

Unmould onto a serving plate. Whip cream until thick, add sherry and pour this sauce over your soufflé. Serve with additional pouring cream.

SERVES 6

HOT CHOCOLATE SOUFFLE

100 g (3½ oz) dark or cooking chocolate
2 tablespoons water
1¼ cups (310 ml/10 fl oz) milk
3 tablespoons caster sugar
2 to 3 drops vanilla essence
1 tablespoon flour
2 teaspoons arrowroot
25 g (1 oz) butter
3 egg yolks
4 egg whites

Preheat the oven to 170°C (325°F).

Prepare a soufflé dish as for Orange and Chocolate Soufflé (see recipe page 44).

Break chocolate into a bowl, add water and stir over a gentle heat until chocolate has melted. Reserve 4 tablespoons milk and add remainder to melted chocolate. Bring to the boil and add sugar and vanilla essence.

Blend reserved milk with flour and arrowroot, stir into chocolate and bring to the boil, stirring continuously. Boil for 2 seconds, draw aside and dot surface with butter. Cover and leave for 5 minutes.

Beat egg yolks into custard one at a time.

Whisk egg whites until stiff and fold into custard. Pour mixture into the soufflé dish and bake for 45 minutes. Remove from oven, undo string and remove paper by holding a knife alongside soufflé dish and peeling paper carefully away. Serve immediately.

SERVES 4

FILO PASTRY

To ensure filo pastry does not dry out when you are using it, cover with a damp tea towel if you are called away from your task for a short while.

POIRE WILLIAM CHOCOLATE TART

6 sheets filo pastry
90 g (3 oz) unsalted butter, melted
3 William or beurre bosc pears
2 tablespoons lemon juice
2 eggs
¼ cup (60 ml/2 fl oz) Poire William or brandy
3 tablespoons icing sugar
2 tablespoons drinking chocolate
¼ teaspoon ground cinnamon
¼ teaspoon nutmeg, freshly grated
90 g (3 oz) chocolate chips
extra icing sugar, to serve

Preheat the oven to 190°C (375°F).

Brush base of a 23 cm (9 in) flan tin liberally with butter. Lay and press in three sheets of filo, brushing each well with butter. Cover remaining filo with a damp tea towel until required.

Trim edges with scissors, to give a ragged finish. Spread filo scraps on a tray so they dry and curl slightly.

Peel, core and thinly slice pears. Sprinkle with lemon juice.

Whisk eggs with remaining ingredients, except chocolate chips, until thick. Stir in chocolate chips.

Arrange half the pear slices in pastry case. Pour half the egg mixture over, then top with remaining filo sheets, brushing each one with melted butter as before. Trim edges and place scraps on a tray to dry slightly. Arrange remaining pears on top, and pour egg mixture over them. Scatter filo trimmings on top to cover the tart, then drizzle with remaining butter.

Bake for about 25 minutes, or until pastry is crisp. If it begins to brown too much, reduce temperature to 180°C (350°F) and cover top loosely with foil.

Cool slightly in tin, then remove ring and slide flan onto a serving plate. Dust with icing sugar just before serving. Serve with thick cream.

SERVES 6 TO 8

Hot Drinks

Hot chocolate drinks evoke a sense of warmth whenever they are served. Whether you prepare them as a rainy afternoon treat or an extravagant end to a dinner party, they will be well received.

CHOCOLATE THICK SHAKE

3 scoops chocolate ice cream
3 tablespoons milk
2 tablespoons chocolate syrup
4 whole marshmellows
2 tablespoons whipped cream

Place all ingredients, except cream, into a saucepan and heat gently, stirring to combine. Alternatively, place all ingredients, except cream, into a large glass or jug. Cook on medium in a microwave for 1 minute, stirring twice during cooking.

Pour into drinking cups and top with whipped cream.

SERVES 2

CHOCOLATE LIQUEURS

Try making hot black coffee, mixing it with your favourite spirit and topping with cream and grated chocolate. Crème de cacao, brandy, whisky and rum are all suitable.

Alternatively, mix chocolate with milk (and maybe some coffee – experiment until you find a taste you like) then pour in your alcohol. These drinks are a great way to finish off a dinner party and make an exciting change from everyday coffee.

HOT MOCHA CHOCOLATE

3 to 4 tablespoons cocoa
2 to 3 tablespoons instant coffee
4 to 6 teaspoons coffee crystals (sugar)
4 cups hot water
whipped cream
chocolate curls

Combine coffee, cocoa and coffee crystals. Boil water in kettle or heat water in jug in a microwave on high for 6 to 8 minutes until almost boiling. Combine with coffee mixture.

Pour into serving cups, top with whipped cream and chocolate curls and serve.

SERVES 6

DRINKING CHOCOLATE

Remember that drinking chocolate and cocoa are not interchangeable: drinking chocolate has a milder, sweeter flavour

Gâteaux

These are really superb, the crème de la crème of the chocolate lovers' repertoire. They may take some time to make, but you will be thrilled by the results — they will look stunning and taste fantastic!

Cake stand and server from The Bay Tree

CHOCOLATE ORANGE GATEAU

ingredients for 1 Genoese sponge (see Cupid's Chocolate Cake recipe, page 55)

75 g (2½ oz) butter

175 g (6 oz) icing sugar

few drops orange essence

1 tablespoon milk

500 g (16 oz) dark or cooking chocolate

Prepare and cook Genoese sponge following instructions in Cupid's Chocolate Cake. Turn sponge out of tin and allow to cool. Cut into 3 equal layers.

Cream butter until soft and beat in icing sugar, a little at a time, until soft and fluffy. Add orange essence and milk, and blend thoroughly.

Measure 40 g (1½ oz) chocolate and melt gently. Beat into buttercream mixture. Divide mixture and spread half over bottom layer and half over middle layer of cake. Place upper layer of cake on top.

Place a bowl in a pan of hot water. Chop remaining chocolate, put it in bowl and stir until it melts. Spread chocolate over top and sides of cake. Decorate cake, if you wish, with whipped cream or bought cake decorations.

SERVES 6 TO 8

GLOSSY CHOCOLATE

Ensure that no water gets into the bowl while melting chocolate (unless this is a part of the recipe). Water prevents a good sheen and will make the chocolate thick.

Pictured on previous pages: Chocolate Ricotta Cake (page 50)

MANDARIN SURPRISE GATEAU

1½ quantities ingredients for Genoese sponge (see Cupid's Chocolate Cake recipe, page 55)

finely-grated rind 1 orange

Filling and Topping

50 g (2 oz) ground almonds

110 g (3½ oz) icing sugar

225 g (7 oz) canned mandarins in syrup

few drops green food colouring

1¼ cups (310 ml/10 fl oz) thickened cream

175 g (6 oz) chocolate, finely grated to form curls

Preheat the oven to 190°C (375°F).

Prepare Genoese sponge following instructions in Cupid's Chocolate Cake, substituting an equal quantity of flour for cocoa powder, and adding orange rind to flour.

Transfer mixture to a greased and lined 25 cm (10 in) cake tin and bake for about 1 hour, until firm to the touch. Turn onto a wire rack to cool.

To Prepare the Filling: Combine almonds and sugar. Drain mandarins, reserve some syrup and add enough syrup to almonds and sugar to form a spreading consistency. Tint with a few drops of green food colouring.

Whip cream until just thick. Reserve 22 mandarin segments for decoration, chop remainder and add to half the cream. Split cold sponge into 3. Spread 2 layers with almond mixture and mandarin cream. Reassemble cake.

Pipe cream over top of cake and decorate with mandarin segments and chocolate curls.

SERVES 12

CHOCOLATE RICOTTA CAKE

Cake

6 eggs, separated

220 g (7 oz) caster sugar

¾ cup (180 ml/6 fl oz) vegetable oil

¾ cup (180 ml/6 fl oz) water

180 g (6 oz) self-raising flour

180 g (6 oz) drinking chocolate

Filling

180 g (6 oz) ricotta

60 g (2 oz) vanilla sugar

2 tablespoons Grand Marnier

30 g (1 oz) preserved ginger, chopped

30 g (1 oz) glacé cherries, quartered

30 g (1 oz) dark or cooking chocolate, roughly chopped

Syrup

2 tablespoons sugar

2 tablespoons Grand Marnier

⅓ cup (85 ml/3 fl oz) water

Icing

90 g (3 oz) dark chocolate

½ cup (125 ml/4 fl oz) water

125 g (4 oz) butter, at room temperature

60 g (2 oz) caster sugar

90 g (3 oz) toasted flaked almonds

Preheat the oven to 180°C (350°F).

To Prepare the Cake: Beat egg yolks with sugar until pale and fluffy. Stir in combined oil and water. Stir in sifted flour and drinking chocolate until thoroughly mixed. Beat egg whites until soft peaks form, then gently fold into chocolate mixture. Pour into a 23 cm (9 in) buttered and base-lined springform pan. Cook for 1 hour. Cool in tin.

To Prepare the Filling: Beat ricotta until smooth, then gradually beat in sugar and Grand Marnier. Fold in remaining ingredients.

To Prepare the Syrup. Combine syrup ingredients in a small saucepan and stir over a low heat until sugar has dissolved.

To Prepare the Icing: Melt chocolate with water. Cool. Beat butter with sugar until pale, then mix in chocolate.

To Assemble the Cake: Cut cake into three horizontal layers. Place one layer on a serving plate, brush with syrup, then spread with half ricotta filling. Top with another cake layer, brush with syrup and spread with remaining filling. Brush cut surface of third cake layer with remaining syrup. Position on top of cake. Spread icing over top and sides of cake, and press almonds around sides with a wide metal spatula. Refrigerate until required.

SERVES 10

DOBOS TORTE

4 eggs, separated

125 g (4 oz) caster sugar

125 g (4 oz) ground hazelnuts

FILLING

125 g (4 oz) unsalted butter

60 g (2 oz) icing sugar, sifted

125 g (4 oz) dark or cooking chocolate, melted

TOPPING

90 g (3 oz) raw sugar

2 tablespoons water

8 whole hazelnuts, roasted, for decoration

Preheat the oven to 180°C (350°F).

Whisk egg yolks and sugar until thick and creamy. Using clean beaters, whisk whites to form stiff peaks. Fold into yolk mixture, alternately with hazelnuts.

Pour mixture into 2 buttered and lined 18 cm (7 in) or 20 cm (8 in) sandwich tins. Bake for 30 minutes, or until firm. Cool in tins for 10 minutes, then turn out onto a wire rack.

To Prepare the Filling: Beat together butter and icing sugar until pale and fluffy, then beat in chocolate.

Place one cake on a serving plate, spread with half filling and position remaining cake on top.

To Prepare the Topping: Heat sugar with water in a small saucepan, stirring until sugar has dissolved. Bring to the boil, and boil without stirring until mixture reaches 176°C (345°F) on a sugar thermometer (caramel stage). Pour onto top of cake and, using an oiled metal spatula, spread quickly and evenly. When caramel is still slightly soft, score top into eight portions with a sharp knife. Position a hazelnut on each slice. Spread remaining icing around sides of cake.

SERVES 8

BLACK FOREST GATEAU

Pictured on page 52.

Soak the cherries overnight in Kirsch for sumptuous results.

6 eggs, separated

250 g (8 oz) sugar

¾ cup (180 ml/6 fl oz) vegetable oil

¾ cup (180 ml/6 fl oz) water

185 g (6 oz) self-raising flour

185 g (6 oz) drinking chocolate

680 g (23 oz) pitted morello cherries

200 g (6½ oz) dark chocolate

1 tablespoon cornflour

¾ cup (180 ml/6 fl oz) Kirsch

2½ cups (625 ml/21 fl oz) thickened cream

caraque (see recipe, page 24) for decoration

icing sugar

Preheat the oven to 180°C (350°F).

To Prepare the Cake: Beat egg yolks with sugar until light and frothy. Add oil and water, beating constantly. Sift flour and drinking chocolate. Add to egg mixture and combine well. Beat egg whites until soft peaks form. Fold into chocolate mixture. Pour into a greased 23 cm (9 in) spring-sided cake tin. Bake for 1 hour. Allow to cool in tin.

To Prepare the Filling: Drain cherries, reserving syrup. Pour Kirsch over cherries, then cover and soak overnight, or as long as possible. Drain again, reserving Kirsch. Combine reserved syrup and cornflour in a small saucepan. Add cherries and cook until thickened. Allow to cool.

To Assemble the Cake: Cut cake in half and brush with reserved Kirsch. Reserve 12 cherries and spread remaining cherry mixture on one cake layer. Place other layer on top and spread both with whipped cream. Cover top and sides with chocolate caraque (see recipe, page 24). Decorate with reserved cherries and dust cake with sifted icing sugar just before serving.

SERVES 8 TO 10

GRATED ORANGE RIND

When grating orange rind, ensure that there is no white pith — this is very bitter.

CHOCOLATE RUM GATEAU

160 g (5 oz) flour

4 tablespoons cocoa powder

½ teaspoon salt

2 teaspoons baking powder

150 g (5 oz) firmly-packed brown sugar

2 eggs, separated

½ cup (125 ml/4 fl oz) oil

½ cup (125 ml/4 fl oz) milk

½ teaspoon vanilla essence

¼ cup (60 ml/2 fl oz) rum

1¼ cups (310 ml/10 fl oz) thickened cream

125 g (4 oz) chocolate, made into curls or caraque (see recipe, page 24)

Preheat the oven to 180°C (350°F).

Sieve together flour, cocoa powder, salt and baking powder in a bowl and stir in sugar. Mix together egg yolks, oil, milk and vanilla essence and beat with flour mixture to form a smooth batter.

Whisk egg whites until stiff and peaking, then fold into batter with a metal spoon.

Divide mixture between two 20 cm (8 in) greased and lined sandwich tins and bake for about 30 minutes until well risen and firm to the touch. Turn out and cool on a wire rack.

Return cold cakes to clean tins and sprinkle with rum. Leave to stand until rum has been absorbed.

Whip cream until is thick. Use a little less than half to sandwich sponges together, then transfer cake to a serving plate. Spread remaining cream over top and sides. Arrange caraque on top of cake.

SERVES 8

Black Forest Gâteau (see recipe page 51)

Chocolate Rum Gâteau

MINT CHOCOLATE GATEAU

ingredients for 1 Genoese sponge (see Cupid's Chocolate Cake recipe, page 55)

2 cups (500 ml/16 fl oz) thickened cream

1 to 2 tablespoons Crème de Menthe (optional)

125 g (4 oz) milk chocolate

thin mint chocolates to decorate

Preheat the oven to 190°C (375°F).

Prepare Genoese sponge following instructions in Cupid's Chocolate Cake recipe. Transfer mixture to 2 greased and lined 20 cm (8 in) shallow cake tins and bake for 25 to 30 minutes. Cool on a wire rack.

Whip cream until just thick and fold in Crème de Menthe, if you are using it. Reserve a little cream for decoration and use the rest to sandwich sponges and to spread around sides.

Melt chocolate in a bowl over a pan of hot, but not boiling, water and spread over top of cake. Pipe a border of rosettes around top of cake with reserved cream.

Press thin mint chocolates onto sides of cake, and decorate top between rosettes with thin mint chocolates cut in half diagonally.

Note: Mint Chocolate Gâteau can also be decorated with coffee-flavoured truffles. Melt 60 g (2 oz) plain chocolate in a bowl over hot but not boiling water, and stir in a little coffee essence to flavour and thicken the chocolate. Then add enough ground almonds to form a stiff paste. Shape mixture into small balls and toss in chocolate vermicelli or cocoa powder.

SERVES 8

MELTED CHOCOLATE

To melt chocolate, place it in a bowl over hot (not boiling) water. Over-heated chocolate has a bitter taste and loses its gloss and aroma.

GATEAU CHOCOLATINE

This gâteau is also based on a Genoese sponge foundation. The decoration is elaborate but it makes the cake a good party piece.

1½ quantities of ingredients for Genoese sponge (see recipe Cupid's Chocolate Cake, p 55)

500 g (16 oz) dark or cooking chocolate

180 g (6 oz) butter, at room temperature

375 g (12 oz) icing sugar

3 tablespoons Grand Marnier

4 tablespoons apricot jam, warmed

½ cup (125 ml/4 fl oz) thickened cream, whipped

Preheat the oven to 190°C (375°F).

Prepare Genoese mixture following the recipe instructions. Pour mixture into a greased and lined 25 cm (10 in) cake tin and bake for 45 minutes or until cooked. Cool on a wire rack.

Prepare a piece of greaseproof paper for chocolate shapes by drawing a circle 6.5 cm (2¾ in) wide, and 16 triangles 8.5 cm (3¼ in) long and 4 cm (1½ in) wide at the widest point.

Grate 125 g (4 oz) chocolate and keep to one side. Break remaining chocolate into a bowl and stand over a pan of hot, but not boiling, water until melted.

Cream butter until light and fluffy. Add icing sugar gradually, beating well, then beat in Grand Marnier. Add a little melted chocolate to flavour and colour it lightly.

Make a greaseproof paper cone, fill with a little melted chocolate and snip the pointed end. Pipe chocolate onto the drawn outlines and fill shapes with chocolate 'squiggles', refilling bag with melted chocolate when necessary. Leave until set.

Split cold sponge into 2 layers and sandwich with apricot jam and whipped cream.

Reserve ⅓ of prepared buttercream for piping and spread rest over top and sides of cake. Press grated chocolate onto sides.

Place reserved buttercream in a piping bag fitted with a star nozzle and pipe 16 large rosettes around top of cake. Remove set chocolate triangles from paper with a palette knife and arrange on cake in a cartwheel fashion, slanting each one on a piped rosette.

Pipe a circle of buttercream around the tip of the chocolate triangles and lay the chocolate circle on top.

SERVES 16

CUPID'S CHOCOLATE CAKE

Genoese Sponge

4 eggs

110 g (3½ oz) caster sugar

75 g (2½ oz) unsalted or clarified butter, cooled

75 g (2½ oz) flour

1 tablespoon cocoa powder

Topping

1¼ cups (310ml/10 fl oz) thickened cream

few drops vanilla essence

250 g (8 oz) milk chocolate

Preheat the oven to 190°C (375°F).

To Make Genoese Sponge: Place eggs and sugar in a basin over a bowl of hot water. Whisk until mixture leaves a trail when you hold up the whisk. Remove from heat and continue whisking until cool.

Sift flour and cocoa together. Gently fold small quantities of flour and melted butter alternately into egg mixture, finishing with flour.

Pour mixture into 2 lined, greased, heart-shaped cake tins. Bake for 25 to 30 minutes, until cooked. Test by lightly touching the centre of the sponge. When cake feels firm and there are no finger marks, it is cooked. Also, sponge should have shrunk away slightly from the sides of the tin. Cool cake on a wire rack.

Whip cream with vanilla. Reserve some whipped cream for decoration and use the rest to sandwich cold sponges.

Make chocolate curls for decoration by scraping a large piece of chocolate bar with a vegetable peeler. Melt remaining chocolate in a bowl over a pan of hot, but not boiling, water and spread over top and sides of cake.

When chocolate has set, pipe cream in a heart shape on top of cake. Pipe three lines of cream from top to bottom of cream heart and top with chocolate curls. Decorate with a red ribbon if you like.

Note: For extra zing, sprinkle 2 tablespoons of rum or Tia Maria over the cooked sponges.

SERVES 6 TO 8

CRUNCHY CHOCOLATE GATEAU

Cream-filled cakes can be messy to cut. This recipe explains how to make life much easier — by cutting the top two layers in advance.

100 g (3½ oz) puffed rice

125 g (4 oz) dark or cooking chocolate

15 g (½ oz) butter

1¼ cups (310 ml/10 fl oz) whipped cream

peppermint essence

green food colouring

mint leaves or geranium leaves to decorate

Melt chocolate in a bowl over hot, not boiling, water. Place puffed rice in a bowl. Pour on melted chocolate and mix well with a metal spoon.

Use butter to grease the bases of three 18 cm (7 in) flan tins. Press puffed rice and chocolate into base of flan rings, making a layer about 6 mm (¼ in) thick.

Using a sharp knife, cut two chocolate bases into 6 portions each. Leave remaining base whole. Place each flan tin in a polythene bag, seal and refrigerate for 5 hours, or overnight.

Remove chocolate flan bases from flan tins. Add 3 drops peppermint essence and 2 drops green food colouring to whipped cream. Mix well so that cream is an even, pale green colour.

Spread half the cream over one whole flan base. Arrange 6 slices of another flan in a circle on top. Spread rest of cream on top. Place remaining 6 flan slices on top, lined up with slices on layer below. Leave a small gap between slices so that cream shows between them.

Decorate gâteau with fresh mint or geranium leaves.

SERVES 6

MELTING CHOCOLATE

Melt chocolate slowly without stirring. Some cooks advocate working it with a palette knife if it is to be used for coating cakes or making chocolate cases because this helps to keep the gloss when it sets. The chocolate should be no more than lukewarm.

MILLED BY
TRADITIONAL
GROWN
STORED
MILLED

Pastries, Pies and Tarts

Now, for something a little different! There are some lovely mixtures of flavours here, with fruit, with nuts, and with a range of pastry types as well. There is something here for any mood and any season.

Bowl from Lifestyle Imports, orange press from The Bay Tree, pastry board from Kitchen Kapers, fabric background from South Pacific Fabrics

CHOUX PASTRY

1¼ cups (310 ml/10 fl oz) water

2 teaspoons caster sugar

100 g (3½ oz) butter

225 g (7 oz) plain flour, sieved

pinch salt

5 to 6 eggs, beaten

Preheat the oven to 200°C (400°F).

In a large saucepan, bring water, sugar and butter to the boil. Remove from heat immediately.

Add sieved flour and salt. Mix well. Return pan to heat and stir continuously until mixture leaves sides of pan. Remove from heat and leave to cool.

Gradually add beaten eggs, mixing well, until paste is of a dropping consistency. Place mixture in a piping bag fitted with a plain nozzle. It is now ready to use.

MAKES 900 G (30 OZ)

PROFITEROLES WITH RUM SAUCE

½ quantity choux pastry (see recipe above)

1¼ cups (310 ml/10 fl oz) thickened cream

1 tablespoon caster sugar

SAUCE

250 g (8 oz) plain chocolate

¼ cup (60 ml/2 fl oz) rum

60 g (2 oz) butter

Preheat the oven to 200° (400°F).

On a greased baking sheet, put 18 heaped teaspoons of choux pastry, well separated. Bake for 20 minutes until well risen and golden brown. Remove from oven, make a small slit in the side of each to allow steam to escape. Return to the oven for 5 minutes to dry out, then cool.

Just before serving, whip cream with sugar until stiff. Using a piping bag, fill each profiterole through its side slit and pile them all on a dish.

To Make the Sauce: Melt chocolate and rum in a bowl over a pan of simmering water. Add butter and mix well. Pour over profiteroles and serve cold.

MAKES 18

CHOCOLATE AND COFFEE ECLAIRS

¾ quantity choux pastry (see recipe above)

CREAM FILLING

4 egg yolks

125 g (4 oz) sugar

4 tablespoons cornflour

3 cups (750 ml/24 fl oz) milk

1 tablespoon cocoa powder

1 tablespoon instant coffee

ICING

225 g (7 oz) icing sugar

4 tablespoons hot water

1 tablespoon cocoa powder or melted dark chocolate

1 tablespoon instant coffee

Preheat the oven to 200°C (400°F).

Using a piping bag, pipe choux pastry in 12 lengths. Bake for 20 minutes, until well risen and golden brown. Remove from oven, make a small slit in each to allow steam to escape. Return to oven for 5 minutes to dry out, then cool.

To Make the Filling: Beat egg yolks, sugar and cornflour in a saucepan. Heat milk to almost boiling, pour onto egg mixture and stir over heat until it thickens. Divide mixture into two and cool. Flavour one half with cocoa mixed to a paste with a little water, and the other with coffee powder, dissolved in a little boiling water.

Mix sifted icing sugar with hot water. Flavour half with cocoa or chocolate and half with coffee powder.

Just before serving, carefully split éclairs open (without separating the halves), fill one half with chocolate filling and the other with coffee. Coat éclairs with icing, half chocolate and half coffee, and decorate with whipped cream.

MAKES 12

CHOCOLATE EGGNOG FLAN

150 g (5 oz) plain flour

3 tablespoons drinking chocolate powder

100 g (3½ oz) butter or margarine, cut into pieces

30 ml (1 fl oz) cold water

FILLING

75 g (2½ oz) caster sugar

2 eggs

30 g (1 oz) flour

1¼ cups (310 ml/10 fl oz) milk

1 teaspoon vanilla essence

⅔ cup (150 ml/5 fl oz) cream

1 tablespoon rum

grated nutmeg

Preheat the oven to 200°C (400°F).

Sift flour and drinking chocolate and add margarine or butter. Rub in until mixture resembles fine breadcrumbs. Mix to a firm dough with water.

Knead dough lightly and roll out to fit a 20 cm (8 in) flan ring. Refrigerate 10 minutes. Bake blind for 20 minutes.

Pictured on previous pages: Chocolate Walnut Tart with Orange Pastry (page 62)

To Make the Filling: Place 50 g (2 oz) sugar in a bowl with 1 egg and 1 egg yolk. Beat well and mix in flour. Warm milk with vanilla essence and pour on egg mixture, stirring. Return mixture to pan and stir over gentle heat until thickened. Cool slightly. Pour into case, then cool and chill.

Whisk remaining egg white until stiff and peaking, then whisk in remaining 25 g (1 oz) sugar. Whip cream with rum and fold gently into egg whites. Spread mixture over filling and sprinkle with nutmeg.

SERVES 6

CHOCOLATE MERINGUE FLAN

Pictured on page 60

- *1 sweet shortcrust pastry flan case, baked blind (see recipe below)*
- *1 tablespoon gelatine*
- *2 tablespoons water*
- *6 tablespoons cornflour*
- *2 tablespoons cocoa powder*
- *220 g (7 oz) caster sugar*
- *3¾ cups (900 ml/30 fl oz) milk*
- *200 g (6½ oz) melted chocolate*
- *60g (2 oz) butter, cut into small pieces*
- *6 egg yolks*
- *few drops vanilla essence*

Meringue

- *3 egg whites*
- *75 g (2½ oz) caster sugar*

Preheat the oven to 200°C (400°F).

Prepare a 23 cm (9 in) flan case and bake it blind. Let it cool.

Dissolve gelatine in water. Blend together cornflour, cocoa powder and sugar. Warm milk and add gradually to cornflour mixture. Add melted chocolate and dissolved gelatine. Return mixture to pan and cook over gentle heat, stirring, until it thickens.

Remove pan from heat. Stir in butter and egg yolks and flavour with vanilla essence. Allow to cool slightly. Pour mixture into flan case. Refrigerate until set.

In another bowl, beat egg whites until stiff. Gradually add sugar. Spoon meringue over chocolate filling. Bake for about 15 minutes until meringue is crisp and golden on top. If meringue browns too quickly, open door slightly for 1 minute and reduce temperature to 180°C (350°F) for remainder of cooking. Cool before serving.

SERVES 6

SWEET SHORTCRUST PASTRY

- *250 g (8 oz) plain flour*
- *pinch salt*
- *125 g (4 oz) butter*
- *60 g (2 oz) caster sugar*
- *1 egg yolk*
- *2 teaspoons lemon juice*
- *2 tablespoons cold water*

Sift flour and salt into a large bowl. Add butter and rub in until mixture resembles fine breadcrumbs. Add sugar and mix.

Make a well in centre of mixture. Add egg yolk, lemon juice and water. Mix to a slightly crumbly, stiff dough. Knead dough lightly.

Cover dough with plastic wrap and chill for 30 minutes before using.

SUFFICIENT FOR 250 G (8 OZ) PASTRY

MINT CHOCOLATE FLAN

- *75 g (2½ oz) bitter chocolate*
- *20 g (½ oz) butter*
- *175 g (6 oz) crushed ginger biscuits*
- *3 egg yolks*
- *100 g (3½ oz) caster sugar*
- *30 ml (1 fl oz) crème de menthe*
- *2 teaspoons powdered gelatine*
- *30 ml (1 fl oz) water*
- *few drops green food colouring*
- *150 ml (5 fl oz) double cream, whipped*

Melt the chocolate and butter in a pan and blend in the biscuit crumbs. Grease a 20 cm (8 in) flan case and spread the crumb mixture evenly over the base and sides, pressing it down firmly. Chill in the refrigerator.

In a bowl, beat together the egg yolks, sugar and creme de menthe until smooth and thick.

Sprinkle gelatine over the water in a small bowl and stand in a pan of hot water. Stir until the gelantine has dissolved. Allow it to cool slightly and gradually beat it into the egg mixture. Fold in the food colouring and the whipped cream. When the mixture is about to set, pour it into the flan crust. Chill until set and serve.

SERVES 6

CHOCOLATE CHESTNUT RING

½ quantity choux pastry (see recipe, page 58)

Filling and Icing

185 g (6 oz) plain chocolate

2 tablespoons water

2 tablespoons rum

2 tablespoons butter

1¼ cups (310 ml/10 fl oz) whipped cream

450 g (15 oz) chestnut purée

75 g (2½ oz) icing sugar

Preheat the oven to 200°C (400°F).

Spoon choux pastry into a 25 cm (10 in) circle on a greased baking sheet. Bake on middle shelf of oven for 45 to 50 minutes, until well risen and crisp. Remove from oven. Make a few small slits in the side to allow steam to escape. Return to oven for 5 minutes to dry out, then cool. Cut in half horizontally, and scoop out any uncooked pastry.

About 1 hour before serving, heat chocolate and water in a saucepan. When chocolate melts, stir in rum and butter. Cool until chocolate begins to thicken. Put bottom half of the choux ring on a rack over a plate. Beat chestnut purée with icing sugar until smooth. Fill ring with chestnut purée mixture. Pipe or spoon whipped cream on top. Replace top half of ring. Carefully spread chocolate icing over top. Remove to a dish. Chill and serve.

Note: These cream rings can also be filled with soft fruit such as peaches, raspberries, strawberries or blackcurrants. Liquidise or sieve the fruit with sugar to make a purée, fold into the whipped cream and use instead of chestnut filling.

SERVES 8

MELTING CHOCOLATE

Chop or break chocolate into small pieces before you melt it so it will melt quickly and evenly.
Do not stir chocolate while it is melting.
Test that the chocolate is melted by dipping the point of a knife into the centre.

Chocolate Meringue Flan (see recipe page 59)

Chocolate Chestnut Ring

CHOCOLATE PECAN PIE

Rich Shortcrust Pastry

250 g (8 oz) cold butter, cut into small pieces

360 g (12 oz) flour

1 teaspoon salt

iced water

icing sugar, to serve

Filling

2 eggs

210 g (7 oz) caster sugar

60 g (2 oz) plain flour, sifted

125 g (4 oz) unsalted butter, melted

180 g (6 oz) chocolate chips

125 g (4 oz) pecan nuts, crushed

1 tablespoon whiskey or brandy

1 teaspoon vanilla

Preheat the oven to 180°C (350°F).

To Prepare the Pastry: Rub butter into combined flour and salt until the mixture resembles coarse breadcrumbs. Sprinkle iced water over mixture, 1 tablespoon at a time, tossing dough with a fork until it begins to clump together. Turn onto a lightly-floured work surface and knead gently to form a ball. Wrap in plastic wrap and chill for 30 minutes before using.

To Make the Filling: Beat eggs until pale and fluffy, then gradually beat in sugar. Fold in flour and butter, then chocolate, nuts, whiskey and vanilla.

Divide pastry in half and roll one piece to line a 23 cm (9 in) pie dish. Pour filling into shell. Roll remaining pastry and cover pie. Trim edges and crimp. Re-roll pastry trimmings to make decorations if desired. Bake for 40 minutes, or until pastry is golden. Serve warm, dusted generously with icing sugar.

SERVES 6 TO 8

CHOCOLATE WALNUT TART WITH ORANGE PASTRY

Pastry

60 g (2 oz) cold butter, cut into 1 cm (½ in) cubes

125 g (4 oz) plain flour

60 g (2 oz) caster sugar

1 teaspoon finely grated orange rind

4 tablespoons orange juice, chilled

Filling

2 eggs

60 g (2 oz) caster or vanilla sugar

250 g (8 oz) walnut pieces

¾ cup (180 ml/6 fl oz) light corn syrup

30 g (1 oz) unsalted butter, melted

2 teaspoons orange flower water

½ teaspoon finely grated orange rind

Decoration

60 g (2 oz) dark or cooking chocolate

To Prepare the Pastry: Cut butter into combined flour and caster sugar until mixture resembles coarse breadcrumbs. Stir in orange rind, then gradually mix in orange juice, stopping when mixture begins to cling together and leave the side of the bowl. (Add iced water if more liquid is required.) Knead gently and shape into a disc. Wrap in plastic wrap and refrigerate it for at least 1 hour, or overnight.

Preheat the oven to 190°C (375°F).

Roll on a lightly-floured surface (this is a soft pastry, so work it gently) to fit a 23 cm (9 in) loose-base tart tin. Lay pastry in tin, pressing gently from the centre out to remove air pockets. Trim edges and patch any thin areas with trim. Freeze for five minutes.

Line with baking paper and fill with baking beans. Place on lower shelf of oven and cook for 15 minutes. Remove beans and paper, reduce temperature to 170°C (300°F) and cook until shell is firm in the centre, about 5 minutes. Remove from oven and cool in tin.

To Prepare the Filling: Whisk together eggs and sugar until pale and fluffy. Stir in remaining ingredients. Place tart pan on a baking tray and pour in filling. Bake for 25 minutes on lower shelf at 180°C (350°F). Transfer to centre oven shelf, reduce heat to 150°C (300°F) and cook for 5 minutes more, or until centre is puffed and feels firm to the touch.

Cool slightly in tin, then unmould onto a serving plate.

For decoration, melt chocolate, place in a piping bag fitted with a writing nozzle (or spoon into a small plastic bag and snip the corner to make as small a hole as possible). Pipe chocolate decoratively over top of tart.

SERVES 8

GLOSSY CHOCOLATE

Ensure that no water gets into the bowl while you are melting chocolate (unless, of course, this is part of the recipe!). Water prevents a good sheen and will make your chocolate thick.

CHOCOLATE PITHIVIERS

500 g (16 oz) puff pastry (commercially produced block puff pastry is suitable)

Filling

60 g (2 oz) blanched almonds, ground

60 g (2 oz) caster sugar

60 g (2 oz) unsalted butter, at room temperature

2 egg yolks

2 tablespoons dark rum

200 g (6½ oz) dark cooking chocolate, chopped

Make the filling the day before required. Beat almonds, sugar, butter and 1 egg yolk until a smooth paste. Beat in rum, then stir in chocolate. Refrigerate.

Roll ⅓ of the pastry on a lightly floured board, to give a 20cm (8 in) circle. Trim edge with a sharp knife, by pressing down, not drawing knife through pastry, as this will compress edges and hamper the puff process. Wet a large baking tray with cold water, shaking off excess. Place pastry circle in centre, cover and chill 30 minutes. Smooth prepared filling over pastry, to within 2.5 cm (1 in) of the edge. Brush border lightly with water. Roll remaining pastry to same diameter but twice the thickness of the base, trimming edges as before. Lay on top of base and press edges together to seal. Press the back of a knife into edge of pastry at 2.5 cm (1 in) intervals, to form a scalloped edge. Cover and chill for 30 minutes.

Preheat oven to 230°C (425°F).

Brush entire top surface of pastry with beaten remaining egg yolk, taking care not to let any drip down sides. Cut a 1 cm (¼ in) hole in centre of top and insert a small tube of rolled aluminium foil. Using a sharp pointed knife, cut lines, about 3 mm (⅛ in) into pastry, starting at the centre point and radiating to the outer edge in a curved crescent shape. Using a metal skewer, pierce right through the pastry in about six places.

Bake in oven for 10 minutes, reduce heat to 200°C (400°F) and bake a further 30 to 40 minutes. About 10 minutes before the end of cooking, remove from oven and sprinkle pithiviers with sifted icing sugar. Return to oven to caramelise. Remove from oven, remove foil tube and cool slightly on baking sheet. Transfer to a wire rack in a draft-free position. Serve lukewarm.

SERVES 6 TO 8

CHOCOLATE, MASCARPONE AND CREAM CHEESE STRUDEL

60 g (2 oz) sultanas

¼ cup (60 ml/2 fl oz) cognac or brandy

100 g (3½ oz) mascarpone

250 g (8 oz) cream cheese, at room temperature

1 tablespoon vanilla sugar

1 egg

200 g (6½ oz) dark cooking chocolate, grated

12 sheets filo pastry

walnut or hazelnut oil, for brushing

icing sugar, for dusting

Sauce

250 g (8 oz) dark cooking chocolate, broken into pieces

¾ cup (180 ml/6 fl oz) cream

2 teaspoons cognac or brandy

Soak sultanas in cognac for at least 1 hour, but preferably overnight.

Preheat oven to 180°C (350°F).

Beat mascarpone with cream cheese, vanilla sugar and egg until smooth and light. Fold in sultanas and cognac, and ½ cup (125 g/4 oz) of the grated chocolate. Lay a clean tea-towel on work surface and place two sheets filo on this. Brush top sheet with oil and sprinkle with some of the remaining grated chocolate. Repeat, brushing and sprinkling every second sheet of filo, until all are used. Spoon mascarpone mixture down centre length of pastry sheets, leaving 5 cm (2 in) free at each end. Fold these ends over filling, then fold long edges over to form a strudel roll. Using the tea-towel to assist, lift strudel onto a baking sheet and bake in oven for 30 to 40 minutes, or until pastry is crisp. Remove from oven and transfer to a serving platter.

To Prepare Sauce: Combine ingredients in the top of a double boiler or a microwave bowl, and heat, stirring frequently, until ingredients are melted and sauce is smooth.

Dust strudel with icing sugar and serve warm, or at room temperature, with sauce passed around separately.

SERVES 8 TO 10

CHOCOLATE ALMOND CREAM FLAN

175 g (6 oz) margarine
75 g (2½ oz) icing sugar
25 g (1 oz) cocoa powder
1 egg, beaten
275 g (9 oz) flour
30 g (1 oz) grated chocolate or caraque (see recipe, page 24)

ALMOND CREAM

1¼ cups (310 ml/10 fl oz) milk
25 g (1 oz) ground almonds
55 g (2 oz) caster sugar
3 tablespoons cornflour
⅓ cup (85 ml/3 fl oz) cream

Preheat the oven to 190°C (375°F).

Cream margarine and sugar together. Beat in cocoa and egg. Blend in flour gradually and knead to a smooth dough. Wrap and refrigerate for 30 minutes.

Lightly grease a 20 cm (8 in) fluted flan tin. Roll out pastry to 5 mm (⅛ in) thick and line tin. Prick pastry base. Bake blind for 25 minutes. Allow to cool.

Meanwhile, bring milk to the boil. Remove from heat. Stir in combined ground almonds, sugar, cornflour and cream to make a smooth, thick mixture. Heat gently, stirring, for 3 to 4 minutes, until well thickened. Allow to cool and pour into the flan case. Chill until set. Sprinkle with grated chocolate or caraque, decorate with toffee almonds (see note), and serve.

Note: To make toffee almonds, put 120 g (4 oz) sugar in a small saucepan. Add 2 to 3 tablespoons of water, dissolve and boil until mixture turns golden. Quickly drop your almonds into it, coat them with toffee, lift them out with a fork and drop them on a greased flat surface to set.

SERVES 6

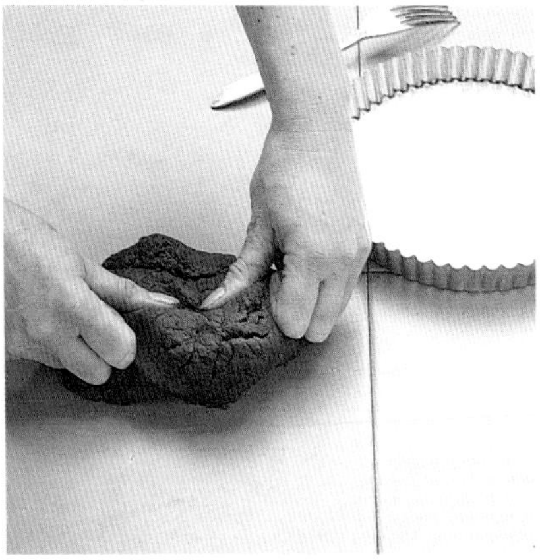

Knead the pastry to form a smooth dough.

Line tin with pastry, prick base with a fork and bake blind.

Pour the almond cream into the flan case.

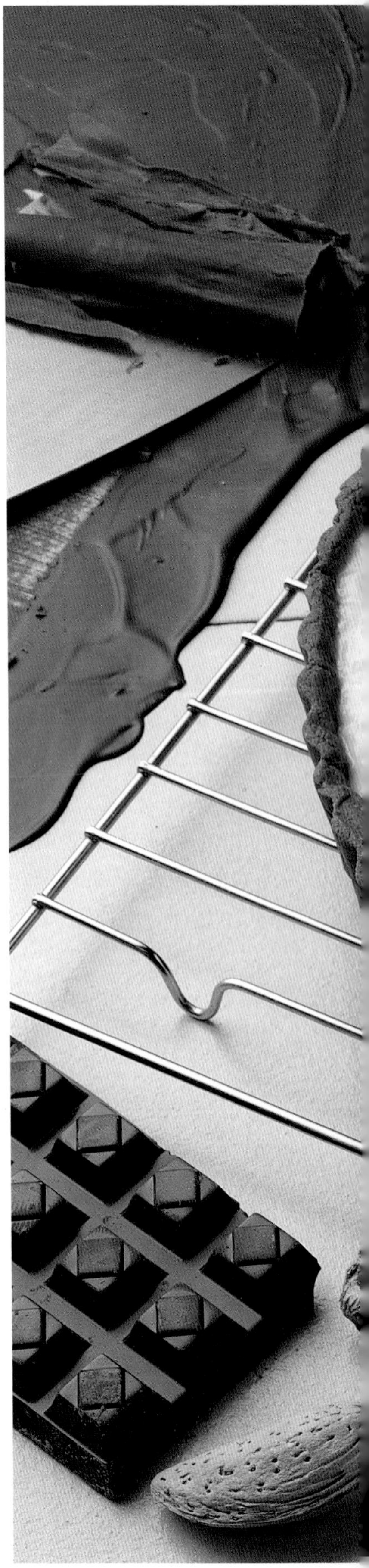

Chocolate Almond Cream Flan

Homemade Confectionery

Homemade confectionery makes a wonderful gift. Suitable for all occasions and all ages it will delight anyone who receives it. In this section you will find all sorts of delicious handmade chocolates and truffles. We have also included a section on wrapping your chocolates to make the perfect present.

French glass balls from The Country Trader, gold cupids from L A Decorative Design

Chocolate-Making Equipment

Double boiler

A two-tiered system of melting chocolate, fillings or delicate sauces without direct contact with heat. A heatproof bowl or saucepan is placed above a saucepan half-filled with hot water. Make sure the water does not come up as high as the bottom of the bowl containing the chocolate.

Bain-marie

A metal vessel half-filled with hot water, in which bowls of chocolate or fillings are gently cooked or melted.

Electric frypan

Useful as a version of the bain-marie, particularly if you want to melt several different types of chocolate or filling at once. Half-fill the frypan with hot water and stand small ceramic heatproof bowls in the water.

Small heatproof bowls

For use in melting chocolate in electric frypans.

Thermometer

Certain recipes, such as fondant, praline and fudge, require careful temperature control. Use a sugar thermometer as it measures the higher temperatures required in chocolate making.

Pictured on previous pages: Apricot Truffles (page 86), Chocolate Cheese Bites (page 86), Port and Pistachio Nut Truffles (page 77), Ten Minute Truffles (page 76), Chestnut Creams (page 81)

Dipping sticks and spoons

Used for dipping pieces of fruit or nuts into melted chocolate to be coated all over.

Oils, colourings and essences

Chocolates can generally only be flavoured with oil-based flavours, colours and essences, because the addition of any water to melted chocolate spoils the appearance, taste and consistency of the finished product. Fine paintbrushes are invaluable for delicate colouring effects.

Moulds

A wide range of moulds are now available so you can make your chocolates shell-shaped, heart-shaped, bell-shaped or flower-shaped — or take your pick from conventional chocolate moulds. See Chocolate Moulding recipe, below, for the best results.

Chocolate Tempering

Chocolate tempering is a process used to prepare pure chocolate liquor for cooking purposes. In all the recipes in this book, compound chocolate has been used, unless otherwise stated. Compound chocolate does not require tempering, is much easier to work with, and gives an equally pleasing result.

However, as this book is devoted to chocolate, it is important to mention chocolate tempering. During tempering, it is essential that not one drop of water should come into contact with the chocolate.

Break the pure chocolate into small pieces and place it in a bowl over hot, not boiling water. Stir occasionally until it is melted and the temperature is 46°C to 48°C (115°F to 118°F). If this temperature is exceeded the chocolate is ruined.

Remove the bowl from the saucepan and set it in iced water, stirring carefully until the chocolate begins to set on the bottom. Then warm the chocolate carefully over hot water (not on stove) until the temperature is 31°C (88°F) for dark chocolate, 29°C (84°F) for milk chocolate or 29°C (84°F) for white chocolate. If the above temperatures are exceeded the tempering process should begin again.

It is only necessary to temper chocolate when using it for moulding or dipping. For any fillings, pure chocolate or cooking chocolate can be used without tempering.

Note: In mid-summer months, compound chocolate will set perfectly well but will not have such a glossy appearance.

Chocolate Moulding

Solid chocolates

1 Fill each mould with melted chocolate and tap it on the table to remove air bubbles.
2 Chill the moulds in the freezer until set (about 3 minutes).
3 Tap the moulds gently to remove the chocolates.

Note: Moulds must be clean and dry.

Filled Chocolates

1 Quarter fill moulds with chocolate.

2 Brush chocolate up the sides, then freeze.

3 Add a small amount of filling.

4 Fill to the top with chocolate.

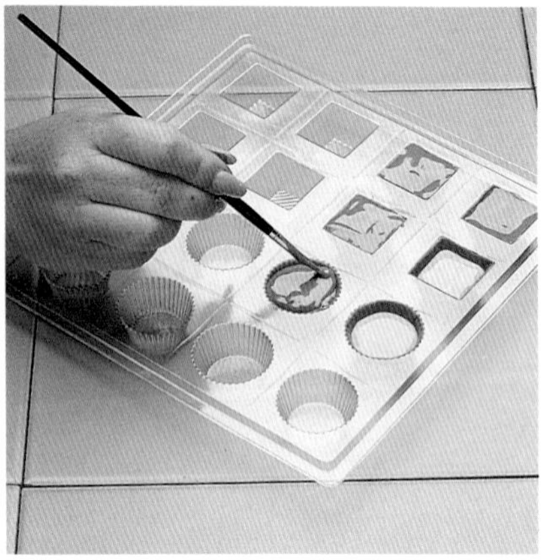

5 Carefully level off the chocolate.

Filled Chocolates

1 Quarter fill the moulds with melted chocolate and tap them to remove air bubbles.
2 Brush chocolate evenly up the sides of the moulds to make a shell and freeze until set (approximately 2 minutes).
3 Add fillings such as truffle, nuts, fondant, fruit, etc.
4 Fill to the top with melted chocolate and tap gently to remove air bubbles.
5 Return to the freezer to set (about 3 minutes), then remove and gently tap out chocolates.

Marbled Chocolates

1 Spoon a little white and dark chocolate separately into a dish.
2 With a teaspoon swirl the white into the dark chocolate to make marble patterns.
3 Gently scoop up some chocolate and fill the moulds evenly.
4 Tap the moulds to remove air bubbles and freeze until set (about 3 minutes). Then tap out the chocolates.

Note: 250 g (8 oz) compound chocolate makes 25 to 30 chocolate shells or 10 to 20 whole chocolates, depending on the size of the mould.

Boiled Fondant

Boiled fondant is the ultimate fondant for chocolate making but it does require a lot of time and care. The simple fondant method (see following recipe) can be used in place of boiled fondant. Boiled fondant is available from certain cake specialty shops.

500 g (16½ oz) granulated crystal sugar

⅓ cup (85 ml/2½ fl oz) water

1 tablespoon liquid glucose

1 Sprinkle a large marble slab or large baking tray with water.
2 Place all ingredients into a saucepan over medium heat and stir, continually brushing down the sides of the saucepan with a wet pastry brush to remove sugar crystals, until sugar dissolves.
3 Bring syrup to the boil over a high heat and continue boiling until a drop of syrup in a saucer of cold water forms a soft ball (approximately 112°C to 116°C (223°F to 240°F)).
4 Remove saucepan from heat and quickly dip base into cold water to stop the cooking.

5 Pour syrup onto prepared marble slab or baking tray and leave to cool for a few moments.

6 With a dampened metal scraper, turn the outsides of the mixture towards the middle to allow mixture to cool evenly. Continue this action until mixture has a yellowish tinge.

7 Using a figure 8 motion, work mixture with a wooden spoon or spatula for 5 to 10 minutes until it becomes opaque, crumbly and white in colour.

8 With wet hands, form mixture into a ball and knead for about 10 minutes until smooth, white and plastic to the touch. Leave covered in the refrigerator overnight for better results.

9 Fondant may be stored indefinitely in an airtight container in the refrigerator.

Alternate Method

Prepare fondant as above, to the end of step 5. When fondant has cooled slightly, beat with a strong electric mixer (ie 350 to 500 watt) until mixture becomes crumbly and white in colour. Then, with wet hands, form mixture into a ball and knead for about 10 minutes, until smooth, white and plastic to the touch. Leave covered in the refrigerator overnight for better results.

Boiled Fondant

1 Brush down the sides of the pan to remove sugar crystals.

2 Test for the soft-ball stage by dropping the mixture into a saucer of water.

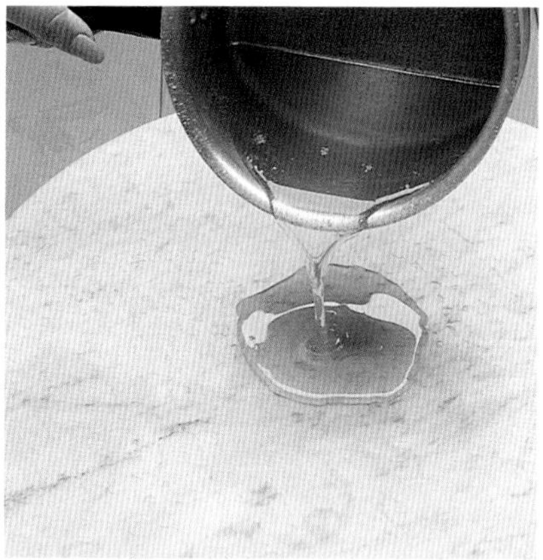

3 Pour the syrup onto the prepared marble slab.

4 Work the mixture with a metal spatula until it thickens.

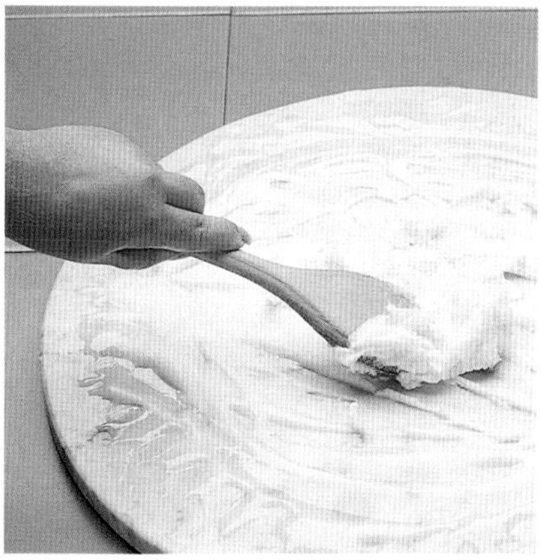

5 Using a wooden spoon, work the mixture in a figure 8 motion until it becomes opaque.

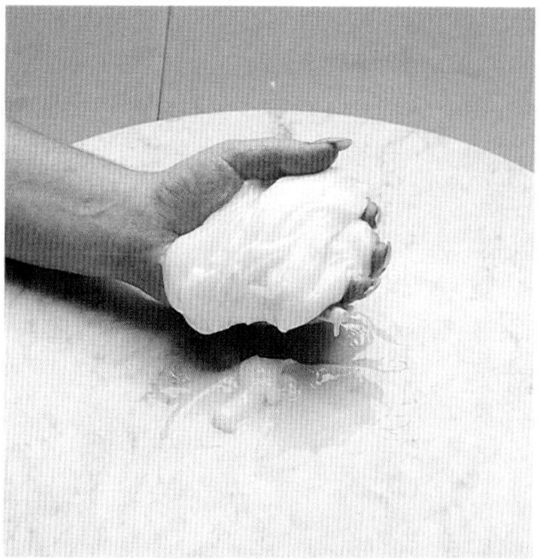

6 Form the mixture into a ball and knead it until it is plastic to the touch.

SIMPLE FONDANT

350 to 375 g (11½ to 12 oz) pure icing sugar

1 egg white

1 tablespoon liquid glucose, warmed

extra icing sugar for kneading

Place icing sugar, egg white and glucose in a bowl and mix together to form a firm paste. Turn paste out onto a board well dredged with extra icing sugar. Knead until dough is easy to handle.

Place in refrigerator in an airtight container.

Add colouring and flavours of your choice and use fondant for fillings and centres for chocolates.

This fondant can also be used for moulding roses and shapes for chocolate decorations.

CHOCOLATE PEPPERMINT LEAVES

Chocolate leaves are the perfect finishing touch for cakes or desserts. They also make an elegant decoration for a plate of chocolates for your dinner party. Choose leaves that are perfect, shiny and heavily veined such as rose, camellia or gardenia leaves, or ivy.

150 g (5 oz) dark compound chocolate

2 to 3 drops peppermint oil flavouring

leaves of your choice

Clean and dry leaves. Melt chocolate by the standard method and add 2 to 3 drops peppermint oil flavouring. Paint the back of each leaf with chocolate, place on a tray and leave to set. Gently peel leaves off chocolate.

1 Melt the chocolate in a small container over hot water.

2 Add the peppermint flavouring.

3 Paint the back of each leaf with chocolate.

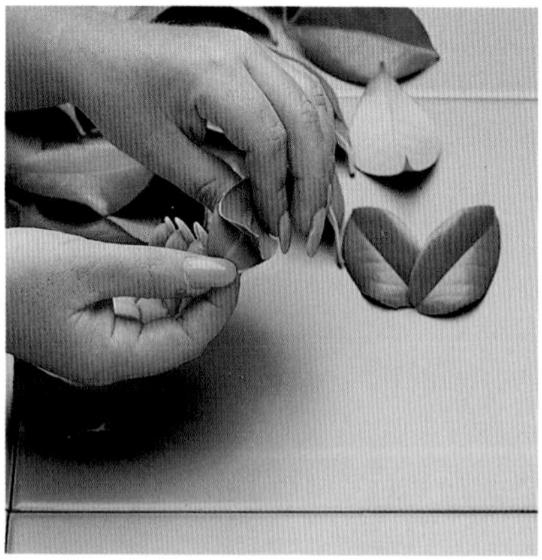

4 When set, gently peel off the leaf.

Chocolate Peppermint Leaves

To vary, use white chocolate coloured with oil-based food colouring and flavoured with other flavours; make pale pink leaves, for instance, with strawberry oil flavouring.

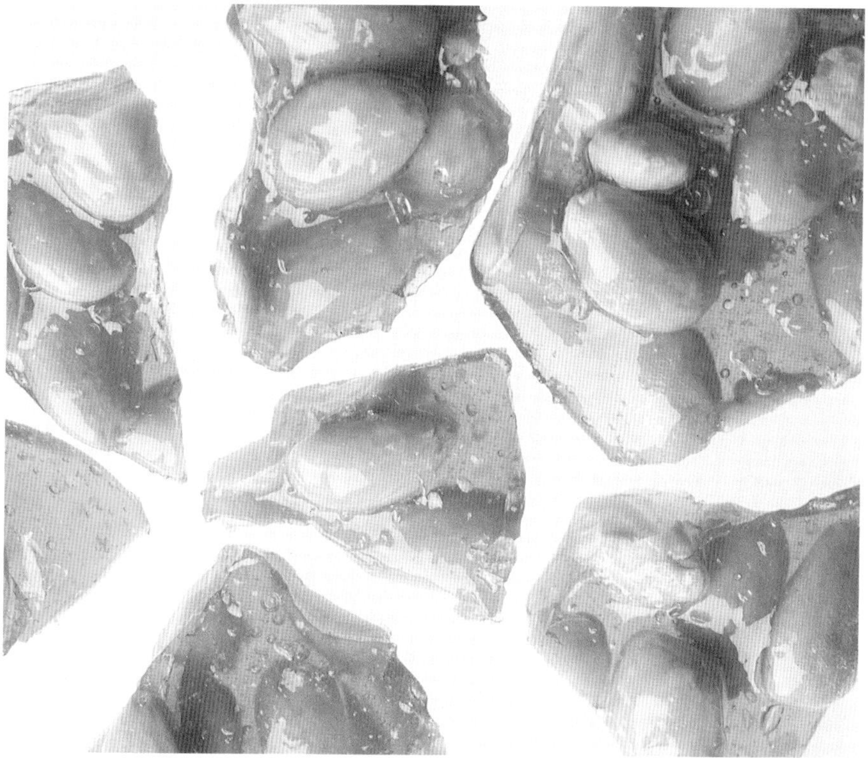

ALMOND PRALINE

350 g (11½ oz) slivered or chopped blanched almonds

⅔ cup (150 ml/5 fl oz) water

500 g (16 oz) granulated sugar

Place almonds on a tray and put into a preheated 180°C (350°F) oven. Switch oven off and leave almonds there to cool (about 15 to 20 minutes).

Thoroughly grease a marble slab or two lamington tins. In a heavy saucepan, over medium heat, dissolve water and sugar, stirring constantly and occasionally brushing down the sides of the saucepan with a wet pastry brush to remove sugar crystals. When sugar has dissolved, allow mixture to boil for 5 to 8 minutes over high heat until a light caramel shade.

Remove saucepan from heat, dip base into cold water immediately, and quickly add warm almonds. Stir gently and pour straight onto greased marble slab or into tins. Allow to cool, break into bite-size pieces and store in an airtight container.

1 *Put almonds in the oven to warm through.*

2 *Dissolve the sugar in the water, stirring and brushing down the sides of the pan.*

3 *Spread the mixture onto a marble slab or cold baking tray.*

4 *When cool, break into bite-sized pieces.*

PRALINE POWDER

This is excellent for chocolate fillings. Place praline pieces into a powerful food processor (350 to 500 watt) and use the strongest blade to reduce the praline to a fine powder. Store in an airtight container.

Note: Ready-made peanut brittle can be used instead of praline. Break the peanut brittle into pieces and use a processor or blender to reduce them to powder.

Wash fruit and pat dry.

Use dipping forks to dip fruit in melted chocolate.

FRUIT DIPPING WITH CHOCOLATE OR FONDANT

500 g (16 oz) berry fruit in season or glacé fruit

½ quantity boiled fondant or simple fondant (see recipe, pages 70-72)

small quantity crystal sugar for coating or 150 g (5 oz) dark compound chocolate, melted

Wash fruit, pat it dry and place it on a tray.

In a large pan, simmer water over medium heat. Put fondant into a smaller pan and place this inside large pan of water. Water should reach as high as the fondant.

Stir fondant continually until it melts. If it is too thick to form an even coat, add a few drops of hot water. Do not heat fondant above 66°C (150°F) or it will become brittle when set.

Holding each piece of fruit by its stalk or by one end, dip it into the fondant. Allow excess fondant to drip off, then dip fondant-coated tip of the fruit into a bowl of sugar. Place on a lined tray and allow to set (approximately 5 to 10 minutes). Any remaining fondant can be re-used.

Fruit can be dipped in melted chocolate instead of fondant and sugar.

Wash the fruit and pat it dry. Use dipping forks to dip the fruit into melted chocolate.

TEN MINUTE TRUFFLES

½ cup (125 ml/4 fl oz) thickened cream

250 g (8 oz) dark cooking chocolate, chopped

2 tablespoons Grand Marnier or cognac

cocoa powder for dusting or crushed nuts for rolling

Heat cream in a saucepan until boiling. Remove from heat. Stir in chopped chocolate until melted. Refrigerate mixture until cool.

Beat mixture at high speed with an electric mixer for 2 to 3 minutes. Add Grand Marnier or cognac. Spoon onto a greased tray and freeze until set. Use as a filling for chocolate moulds, or roll into balls and dust with cocoa powder, or roll in crushed nuts.

CHOCOLATE HAZELNUT FUDGE

90 g (3 oz) compound chocolate

90 g (3 oz) unsalted butter or margarine

1 x 400 g (13 oz) can sweetened condensed milk

2 tablespoons golden syrup

75 g (2½ oz) roasted, chopped, unsalted hazelnuts OR desiccated coconut

150 g (5 oz) dark compound chocolate, melted for coating chocolates

Place all ingredients except hazelnuts into a saucepan and stir over low heat until melted. Bring to the boil, reduce heat and simmer for 15 minutes, stirring constantly until mixture has thickened.

Add chopped hazelnuts, mix well and pour mixture into a greased square tin or bar tin. Refrigerate until firm.

Remove from tin and cut into squares or other shapes, or roll into balls and coat with hazelnut or coconut.

Dip in melted chocolate, then place on a lined tray and allow to set.

Ten Minute Truffles

CHOCOLATE CREAM

To melt chocolate in fresh cream, heat the cream in a heavy-based saucepan on a low heat. Add pieces of chocolate and stir until it is just melted. Allow to cool then beat it by hand or with an electric beater. Use immediately, before it hardens, to cover cakes or desserts.

PORT AND PISTACHIO NUT TRUFFLES

150 g (5 oz) dark compound chocolate

3 tablespoons unsalted butter

75 g ($2\frac{1}{2}$ oz) pure icing sugar, sifted

1 egg yolk

3 tablespoons port

50 g (2 oz) unsalted pistachio nuts, chopped

150 g (5 oz) melted chocolate or additional crushed pistachio nuts

Melt chocolate over hot, not boiling, water. Cream butter and sugar. Allow chocolate to cool and add to butter and sugar mixture, stirring vigorously. Add egg yolk and port and beat until thick and creamy. Stir in nuts, spoon onto greaseproof paper and refrigerate until firm.

Use as a filling for chocolate moulds, or roll into balls and dip in melted chocolate or crushed pistachio nuts.

Above: Port and Pistachio Nut Truffles

Below: Chocolate Hazelnut Fudge

LEMON COCONUT TRUFFLES

½ cup (125 ml/4 fl oz) thickened cream

250 g (8 oz) white compound chocolate, chopped

3 teaspoons freshly grated lemon rind

135 g (4½ oz) desiccated coconut

8 drops lemon food colouring

3 teaspoons milk

Bring cream slowly to the boil, stirring continuously. Remove pan from heat and stir in chopped chocolate. Let this stand until cool, about 30 minutes, then beat with an electric mixer until light and smooth. Blend in lemon rind and 45 g (1½ oz) coconut.

Place teaspoonfuls of mixture on a foil-lined tray and freeze until hard. Add lemon colouring to milk. Put remaining coconut in a plastic bag, add coloured milk and shake vigorously. Roll truffle mixture into balls or pipe it into shapes and roll them in coloured coconut. Keep refrigerated.

Lemon Coconut Truffles

CHERRY LIQUEURS

200 g (6½ oz) fresh cherries or glacé cherries

¼ bottle Kirsch or liqueur of your choice

200 g (6½ oz) dark compound chocolate

1 teaspoon invertase (see note)

250 g (8 oz) boiled fondant or simple fondant (see recipes, pages 70-72)

Prick cherries and soak them in Kirsch or other liqueur for 2 hours or, preferably, overnight. Cherries do not need to be completely covered. Drain and dry thoroughly on paper towels. Excess Kirsch can be re-used.

Add invertase to fondant and wrap fondant around the cherries. Dip all this in melted chocolate and, when set, dip again in melted chocolate to completely seal fondant.

Allow 5 days to liquidise. Serve in paper cases.

Note: Invertase is available from certain department stores and cake specialty shops.

Cherry Liqueurs

1 Bring the cream to the boil, stirring constantly.

2 Add the cooled cream to the chocolate.

3 Add the praline mixture.

4 Roll the mixture into balls and wrap around the hazelnuts.

5 Dip in the melted chocolate.

Hazelnut Truffles sandwiched between moulded chocolate shells

HAZELNUT TRUFFLES

250 g (8 oz) dark compound chocolate

½ cup (125 ml/4 fl oz) thickened cream

1 teaspoon vanilla essence

60 g (2 oz) praline powder (see Almond Praline recipe, page 73) or 60 g (2 oz) chopped, unsalted, roasted hazelnuts

20 to 24 whole, roasted hazelnuts

210 g (7 oz) dark compound chocolate for dipping

Chop chocolate and put it in a bowl over hot water, stirring occasionally until melted. Heat cream in a saucepan until boiling, stirring constantly. Remove cream from heat and cool to room temperature. Stir cream and vanilla essence into melted, cooled chocolate and allow to stand for about half an hour. Beat mixture with an electric mixer until fluffy and lighter in colour.

Fold in praline powder (or chopped hazelnuts) and refrigerate for 30 minutes. Roll mixture into balls around each hazelnut and place on a lined tray. Melt additional chocolate, coat truffles and allow to set on the tray. Alternatively, sandwich truffles between moulded shells, or use truffle to fill chocolate moulds.

ALESSI

CHESTNUT CREAMS

60 g (2 oz) compound chocolate or cooking chocolate, chopped

60 g (2 oz) copha, chopped

60 g (2 oz) unsalted butter, at room temperature

125 g (4 oz) sweetened chestnut spread

2 teaspoons rum

125 g (4 oz) milk compound chocolate (additional)

Melt chocolate and copha over hot water, remove and allow to cool without setting.

Cream butter and beat in chestnut spread and rum. Stir in cooled chocolate mixture.

Melt additional chocolate over hot water. Place 36 coloured foil cases on a tray and pour ½ teaspoon melted chocolate into each case, just enough to cover base. Reserve remaining melted chocolate.

Place chestnut mixture into a piping bag fitted with a fluted tube and pipe swirls of mixture into foil cases.

Trickle reserved melted chocolate over chestnut mixture in cases. Refrigerate until required.

CHOPPING CHOCOLATE

The easiest way to chop chocolate is to break the slab into smallish pieces on a large board. Press down on the back of the knife blade as you chop.

Chestnut Creams and Crunchy Chocolate Squares

CRUNCHY CHOCOLATE SQUARES

250 g (8 oz) milk or dark compound chocolate

90 g (3 oz) praline powder (see Almond Praline recipe, page 73)

Melt chocolate over hot water. Fold in praline powder. Place in square moulds and refrigerate until set. Turn out of moulds and store.

Note: With the addition of praline powder the chocolate mixture will need to be spooned into moulds as quickly as possible as it will be thicker and will set more quickly. Bang the moulds on the bench to spread the mixture evenly.

QUICK AND EASY CHOCOLATE GINGER

½ quantity boiled fondant or simple fondant (see recipe, pages 70-72)

150 g (5 oz) dark chocolate, melted

20 pieces crystallised ginger

Wrap fondant around each piece of ginger. Freeze for 10 minutes until firm. Dip in melted chocolate.

Below: Chocolate Ginger

PASSIONFRUIT CREAMS

210 g (7 oz) condensed milk

2 passionfruit

500 g (16 oz) icing sugar, sifted

150 g (5 oz) dark or white compound chocolate

Combine condensed milk, passionfruit pulp and 400 g (13½ oz) icing sugar. Mix well to form a firm dough. On a board, thoroughly knead mixture into remaining icing sugar. If mixture is not firm enough to roll into balls, add more icing sugar.

Roll into small balls (big enough to fit into chocolate cases) and refrigerate for 30 minutes.

Melt chocolate and use it to coat foil cases or moulds. Refrigerate until set. If using foil cases, remove them from the chocolate when set. Place passionfruit balls into chocolate cases or moulds and refrigerate.

COOLING CHOCOLATE

Cool chocolate at room temperature. This helps to maintain the gloss.

CHOCOLATE PEPPERMINT SHELLS

175 g (6 oz) dark compound chocolate, chopped

60 g (2 oz) unsalted butter, cut into small pieces

2 egg yolks, lightly beaten

3 drops peppermint oil flavouring

150 g (5 oz) dark compound chocolate (additional)

Place chopped dark compound chocolate in a bowl over a saucepan of hot water, and stir until completely melted. Remove bowl and gradually blend in butter, stirring well after each addition.

Blend a little chocolate mixture with beaten egg yolks and then add rest of egg yolks. Stir mixture gently over hot water on a very low heat for 3 to 4 minutes. Add peppermint oil.

Place mixture in freezer for 5 minutes. Remove and allow to set at room temperature.

MOULDING

Brush each shell mould with additional melted chocolate and refrigerate until set.

Fill each shell with the chocolate peppermint mixture, allowing enough space to top with melted chocolate. Reserve the remaining mixture. Cover the top of each mould with melted chocolate and refrigerate until set. Remove the chocolates from their moulds.

Cement each pair of shells together with the remaining chocolate mixture and decorate.

CHOCOLATE CANDY PEEL WITH COINTREAU

2 oranges

300 g (10 oz) sugar

1¼ cups (310 ml/10 fl oz) water

125 ml (4 fl oz) Cointreau

90 g (3 oz) dark or cooking chocolate, melted

Cut orange into quarters. Peel off skin and discard flesh. Remove all pith with a very sharp knife. Cut skin into long strips and rinse under cold running water.

Bring sugar, water and Cointreau to the boil. Add orange strips and simmer for at least 2 hours. Add a little hot water if syrup becomes frothy. Lift out strips onto a cooking rack and flatten them with a spatula. Leave to crystallise for 3 hours or, preferably, overnight. Dip strips in melted chocolate and place on a foil-lined tray to set. Store remaining strips in an airtight jar until you are ready to use them.

CANDIED PEEL

Prepare candied peel in your microwave oven by placing thin strips of peel from 2 oranges or lemons (or 1 of each) in a microwave-safe bowl with 125 g (4 oz) caster sugar and ½ cup (125 ml/4 fl oz) water. Cook on HIGH (100%) power for 3 minutes or until liquid is syrupy. Drain off syrup. Toss peel in some extra caster sugar. When cool, store in an airtight container.

HAZELNUT COFFEE CLUSTERS

150 g (5 oz) chocolate

coffee oil flavouring, to taste

90 g (3 oz) hazelnuts

Melt chocolate over hot, not boiling, water. Add coffee essence. Cement three hazelnuts together at a time with melted chocolate. Allow clusters to set then dip in melted chocolate. Decorate with a hazelnut on top.

MELTING CHOCOLATE

If chocolate is not melting easily, add a little copha (about 2 to 3 per cent of the weight of the chocolate). However, this can increase the 'snap' quality of the chocolate so that a chocolate coating on a cake may not cut quite so neatly.

CHOCOLATE MARZIPAN ROLL

1 quantity marzipan (see below) or 400 g (13 oz) rolled marzipan

125 g (4 oz) dark compound chocolate

orange oil flavouring (optional)

If using homemade marzipan, divide your paste into two and roll out into 2 rectangles about 3 mm (⅛ in) in thickness. Melt chocolate, add orange oil and spread thinly over marzipan shapes, leaving 5 cm (2 in) around edges. Spread only a thin layer of chocolate over marzipan as it will be difficult to roll if it is too thick.

Rolling must be done as chocolate is setting. If allowed to set, chocolate will crack when rolling. Start from the longest side of the rectangle, and roll firmly towards the other longest side.

Wrap marzipan roll in foil and place it in refrigerator for 20 minutes. Trim ends and slice roll with a sawing motion into 5 mm (2 in) pieces, using a serrated knife.

Note: Rolled marzipan is available at certain supermarkets.

MARZIPAN

200 g (6½ oz) icing sugar

200 g (6½ oz) almond meal (ground almonds)

2 egg whites

Sift icing sugar into a bowl and mix in ground almonds.

Beat egg whites until they begin to foam and cut into sifted icing sugar and almonds a little at a time, adding just enough to combine mixture. Work mixture together, adding a little more egg white if it feels too dry or a little more icing sugar if too moist. Knead paste lightly until it comes away from sides of bowl.

EASTER EGGS AND CHOCOLATE BOXES

Cut the mould into two for easy handling. Clean and dry your moulds thoroughly.

Fill both halves of mould with melted chocolate and freeze until outside edge has hardened (about 3 to 4 minutes). Pour out liquid chocolate and set aside. Return mould to the freezer to set. Excess chocolate can be used for further moulding or will keep for a later date.

To join the halves, cement edges together with a little melted chocolate, or pipe edges with melted chocolate or royal icing using a piping bag with a fluted tube.

Before joining halves together, eggs may be filled with small eggs or chocolates.

This method can be used for making chocolate boxes.

Note: The quantity of chocolate depends on the size of your moulds and the number of eggs or boxes required.

GLOSSY CHOCOLATE

Ensure that no water gets into the bowl while you are melting chocolate (unless this is a part of the recipe!). Water prevents a good sheen and will make the chocolate thick.

WHITE CHOCOLATE NUT FUDGE

500 g (16 oz) granulated sugar

1¼ cups (310 ml/10 fl oz) sour cream

90 g (3 oz) white compound chocolate, chopped

½ teaspoon salt

2 tablespoons liquid glucose or light corn syrup

1 teaspoon vanilla essence

10 g (⅓ oz) unsalted butter

60 g (2 oz) unsalted macadamia nuts, chopped

In large, heavy-based saucepan, combine sugar, sour cream, chopped chocolate, salt and liquid glucose or syrup. Stir over low heat until chocolate is melted and sugar has dissolved. Bring mixture to the boil, reduce heat and simmer, covered, for 3 minutes.

Remove lid from saucepan and stir frequently until mixture reaches 118°C (245°F)on a sugar thermpmeter, or soft-ball stage (about ½ an hour). Remove from heat and stir in vanilla and butter. Allow to cool without stirring until lukewarm, then beat vigorously with a wooden spoon until fudge is no longer glossy.

Stir in chopped macadamia nuts and press mixture into a square tin or bar tin lined with aluminium foil, or use nut-shaped moulds. Refrigerate until firm. Unmould or cut into squares.

Note: Other unsalted nuts such as peanuts, hazelnuts or walnuts can be substituted for macadamia nuts.

White Chocolate Nut Fudge used to fill a nut-shaped mould

1 Combine the sugar, sour cream, chopped chocolate, salt and liquid glucose.

2 Stir over low heat until dissolved.

3 Bring to the boil and simmer until the mixture reaches soft-ball stage.

4 Stir in the vanilla and butter.

5 When lukewarm, beat vigorously with a wooden spoon until the fudge loses its gloss.

6 Add the chopped nuts.

7 Press the mixture into a lined tin.

8 When set, cut into squares.

APRICOT TRUFFLES

400 g (13 oz) white compound chocolate

½ cup (125 ml/4 fl oz) thickened cream

60 g (2 oz) glacé apricots

1 teaspoon vanilla essence

3 teaspoons apricot essence

Chop 250 g (8 oz) chocolate and put it in a bowl over hot water. Stir occasionally until melted.

Place cream in a saucepan on the stove and bring to the boil, stirring constantly. Remove from stove and cool to room temperature. Mix cooled cream into melted, cooled chocolate and allow mixture to stand for 20 minutes. Then beat with an electric mixer until mixture is fluffy and lighter in colour. Fold in chopped glacé apricots, vanilla essence and apricot essence.

Refrigerate mixture until firm enough to roll into balls. Shape into small balls and place them on a foil-lined tray. Refrigerate.

Melt remaining 150 g (5 oz) chocolate. Dip truffles in chocolate. Place on the tray to set.

LEMON JUICE

To extract the maximum amount of juice from a lemon, cook in the microwave on HIGH (100%) power for 20 seconds or ensure they are at room temperature and roll on the bench for a few minutes before squeezing.

CHOCOLATE CHEESE BITES

360 g (12 oz) farmer's cheese (a firm cottage cheese sold at specialty cheese shops)

125 g (4 oz) cream cheese

7 tablespoons vanilla sugar

2 egg yolks, lightly beaten

finely grated rind 2 medium lemons

1 tablespoon lemon juice

1½ teaspoons lemon essence

360 g (12 oz) dark or cooking chocolate

3 tablespoons copha

Combine cheeses, sugar and egg yolks in a food processor until smooth. Transfer to a bowl and stir in lemon rind and juice and lemon essence. Line a colander with gauze or dispensable cloth, spoon in mixture and fold cloth over. Cover with a plate and weigh down. Refrigerate for several hours or overnight. Form mixture into 2½ cm (1 in) balls with your hands. Place on a foil-lined tray and freeze for 40 minutes.

Melt chocolate and copha, stirring until smooth. Cool slightly. Remove cheese balls from freezer. Insert a toothpick into the centre of one, dip it in chocolate and replace it on the tray. Twist out toothpick as chocolate hardens. Repeat until all balls are dipped. Spoon remaining chocolate (it may need to be re-warmed slightly at this stage) into a piping bag fitted with a writing nozzle (or a small plastic bag with a tiny snip in one corner) and decorate chocolate balls with a drizzle of chocolate, covering the toothpick hole in the process. (White or milk chocolate can be used for this if you prefer.)

MAKES ABOUT 40

ZEST

The outer layer of citrus fruit skin is known as zest. It may be removed by using a grater (ensure only the colour of the skin is removed, as the white pith underneath is very bitter) or may be peeled off using a vegetable peeler. These pieces of skin may be sliced thinly, blanched and used in recipes. A zester will make even finer strips, and this peel does not require blanching.

MICROWAVE CHOCOLATE TRUFFLES

150 g (5 oz) butter

300 g (10 oz) milk chocolate

1 tablespoon rum

¼ cup (60 ml/2 fl oz) sour cream

60 g (2 oz) chocolate, grated

Break up chocolate. Place butter, chocolate and rum into a 2 litre (3½ pint) mixing bowl. Cook on high for 3 to 4 minutes. Stir to melt chocolate. Fold in sour cream. Pour mixture into a shallow dish. Allow to chill for 1 hour in refrigerator.

Quickly spoon 1 teaspoon of mixture onto grated chocolate, working to form a small ball. Coat with extra grated chocolate. Chill till set.

CHOCOLATE PRALINE CINNAMON BALLS

250 g (8 oz) white compound chocolate

½ cup (125 ml/4 fl oz) thickened cream

90 g (3 oz) praline powder (see Almond Praline recipe, page 73)

1 teaspoon vanilla essence

2 teaspoons cinnamon

100 g (3½ oz) granulated sugar

Chop chocolate into pieces and put them in a bowl. Melt chocolate over hot water, stirring occasionally. Heat cream in a saucepan until boiling, stirring constantly. Remove from heat and cool to room temperature.

Combine with melted chocolate and allow to cool for 30 minutes, then beat with an electric mixer until mixture is fluffy and lighter in colour. Fold in praline powder and vanilla essence. Refrigerate mixture until firm enough to roll into balls.

Mix cinnamon and sugar together. Shape heaped teaspoons of praline mixture into small balls and coat them with cinnamon and sugar.

MELTED CHOCOLATE

To melt chocolate, place it in a bowl over hot, not boiling, water. Over-heated chocolate has a bitter taste and loses its gloss.

DALE'S DELIGHT

1½ cups (375 ml/12 fl oz) light corn syrup

250 g (8 oz) granulated sugar

400 g (13 oz) tin sweetened condensed milk

1¾ cups (450 ml/15 fl oz) thickened cream

90 g (3 oz) unsweetened compound chocolate, chopped

Line a 20 cm (8 in) square tin with foil, then grease. Combine all ingredients except chocolate in a heavy saucepan and place over medium heat, stirring constantly with a wooden spoon until all sugar crystals are dissolved.

Continue cooking for about 45 minutes at 107°C (225°F), stirring frequently. Add chopped chocolate and cook for another 10 to 15 minutes, brushing down the exposed sides of the saucepan with a wet pastry brush while stirring frequently.

Remove from heat and pour into prepared tin. Allow to firm overnight in the refrigerator. Turn out, peel off foil and cut into shapes.

SIMPLE STRAWBERRY CREAMS

90 g (3 oz) Philadelphia cream cheese, at room temperature

200 g (6½ oz) pure icing sugar

3 drops strawberry essence

2 drops pink liquid food colouring

½ teaspoon vanilla essence

150 g (5 oz) compound chocolate, for moulding

Beat cream cheese and icing sugar until smooth. Add strawberry essence, colouring and vanilla.

Melt chocolate over hot, not boiling water. Line a mould with chocolate, freeze, and when set fill it with strawberry cream.

Seal top with chocolate and freeze again until set.

Note: This is an ideal easy method for soft-centred chocolates. Any flavouring and colouring can be used.

COOLING CHOCOLATE

Cool chocolate at room temperature. This helps to maintain the gloss.

Picture Perfect Presents

Friends and family will be delighted to receive a gift of handmade confectionery. Few people can resist chocolates and the recipes in this chapter offer a wide variety to choose from.

Many beautiful wrapping papers, boxes, bags and bows are available in stores. Alternatively you can continue the handmade theme and present your gift in wrappings you have created yourself.

You will need to collect a supply of materials so that you always have the ingredients for the perfect package on hand.

Many everyday items can be transformed into wonderful containers for your delicious homemade goodies:

- jars of all shapes and sizes
- shoe boxes
- any small boxes such as those that perfumes, make up and teas come in
- baskets
- cardboard cylinders from lunchwraps or paper kitchen towels
- brandy balloons
- plastic airtight containers that can be re-used by the recipient
- plant pots that become an addition to the present.

Keep an eye out for these items and keep them in your wrapping store.

You might also like to have:

- lace
- ribbons – material ribbons (velvet, satin and grosgrain are great for tying gifts) as well as manufactured gift tying ribbons bought from stationery shops
- glue
- scissors
- large sheets of coloured cardboard
- a variety of pens and pencils – textas, coloured pencils, highlight pens, gold and silver pens

WINTON
21
OIL COLOUR
WINSOR & NEWTON
37ml
HOBBY GLUE
ARTS & CRAFTS
PVA ADHESIVE
50ml
ROYMAC SERIES
JAPAN

- letraset or stick-on letters
- pretty stickers (many varieties are available from coloured spots and gold stars to metallic and picture stickers)
- sticky tape
- double sided sticky tape
- ruler
- stapler
- hole punch
- wrapping papers including tissue paper, cellophane, patterned papers or even plain brown or white paper that you can decorate yourself
- string
- raffia
- paper doilies
- glitter
- scraps of material
- sturdy brown paper lunch bags
- dried flowers and leaves from your garden
- a recent family photograph.

A JAR OF GEMS

Fill a glass jar with your sweet treats. You can either wrap the whole jar or make a pretty 'hat' for it.

To Wrap the Whole Jar: Place the jar on a large square of wrapping paper. Bring each of the four corners of the paper up and tie them at the top of the jar with a lovely bow.

To Make a Hat: Cut a circle of material wider than the lid of your jar. Lay the material over the lid and fasten around the neck of the jar with a ribbon.

A BEAUTIFUL BOX

Take material or paper of your choice and cover the outside and lid of a box separately. You can line the inside with the same or a co-ordinating material.

Place your chocolates in nests of tissue paper or cellophane or on a paper doily.

Pop the lid on the box and decorate with a bow.

A BOUNTIFUL BASKET

Line a basket with layers of tissue paper and lay your gifts in the basket. Take a large piece of cellophane and wrap the whole basket, securing it with a bow at the handle. Alternatively, you can wrap the chocolates in a cellophane bundle and put this inside the basket. Tie a bow around the handle.

A CYLINDER OF SWEETS

Fill a cardboard cylinder (from a roll of lunch wrap or paper kitchen towels) with handmade sweets and wrap up like a bon-bon. Tie each end with ribbon.

MAKING YOUR OWN CARDS

You can make your card any shape you like – circle, triangle, heart. Using coloured cardboard or sturdy paper of your choice cut and fold your card into an appropriate shape. If you would rather make a gift tag you can cut the cardboard to size. Alternatively, small cards can be purchased from stationery stores.

You can either write your message straight onto the card or fold a piece of paper and slot it into the card so that it forms the 'pages' in the 'book'. Secure the paper in place with a ribbon.

The ways of decorating cards are limitless:

- dried leaves and flowers
- children can draw a picture onto the cardboard
- a recent family photograph can be stuck onto the front of the card
- the recipient's name can be written on the card with a fancy pen or letraset
- if the gift is for a cat lover try getting your pet to 'sign' the card with a paw print
- glitter, sequins, stickers and lace can be used to make a colourful collage
- write the recipe for the chocolates on the card in a nice print
- if the present is for a lover you can seal the card with a lipstick 'kiss'
- write love poems or humorous poems you have penned yourself, on the card
- write your message on a scroll made from pretty paper, roll up and tie with a bow.

You can use these ideas to decorate plain wrapping paper.

Making a Gift Bag

You can make your bag out of any sturdy paper you like.

For a natural look try brown paper and use raffia, thick string or a wide dark green ribbon as the handle.

Pretty wrapping papers also make great gift bags. Choose a co-ordinating ribbon for the handle.

At Christmas time, make the bags from Christmas wrapping paper and hang from the branches of your tree as irresistible Christmas decorations.

1 Lay the paper of your choice (pattern side down) on the table.
2 Fold the top of your paper over a short way (say 2 cm/¾ in) to give the top of the bag a neat appearance.
3 Repeat this procedure down one side of the paper.
4 Roll the paper into a cylindrical shape, overlap the ends and glue them together making sure that your neat folded side is on the outside.
5 Lay the bag flat with the seam at the back or at the side (whichever you prefer).
6 Make a fold about 3 cm (1¼ in) from the bottom of the bag.
7 Take the top piece of this fold and flatten out, forming points at each end.
8 Bring the edges of the paper together and glue them securely.
9 Open the bag out and punch holes in the top.
10 Tie ribbon of your choice through the holes to form the handle.

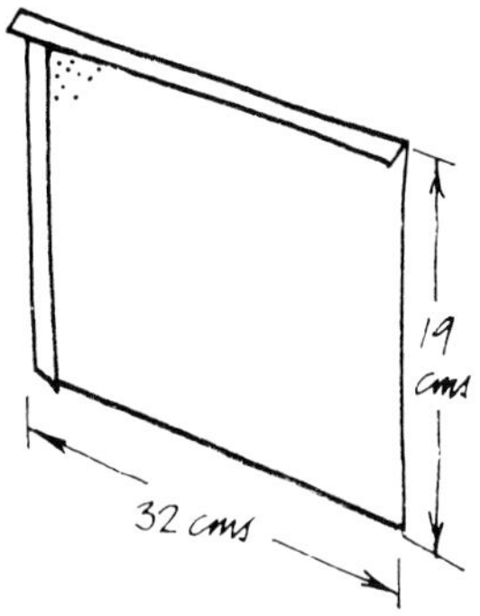

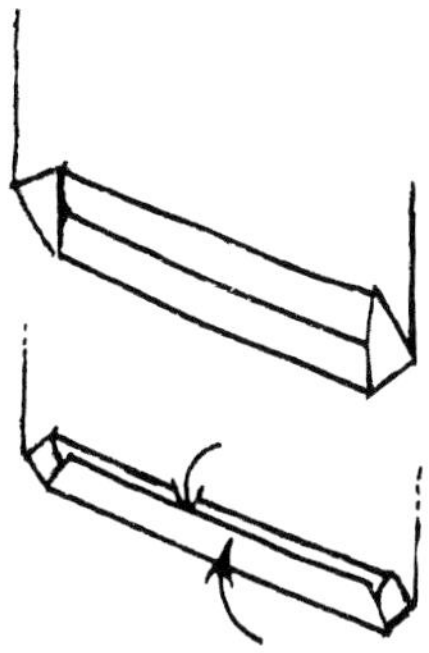

Open out and fold back half of the base ... flatten triangular points

Further fold down and up. Tape overlap

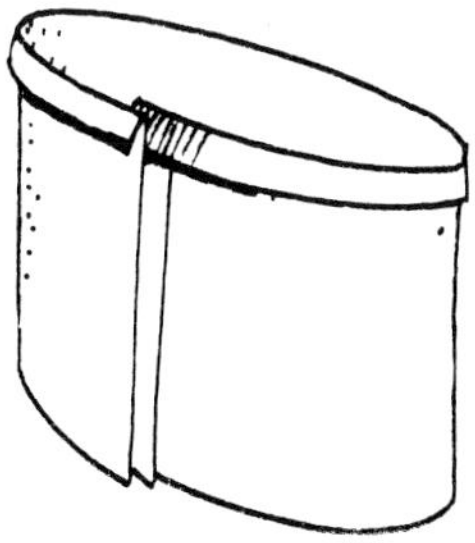

Make a cylinder tape overlap

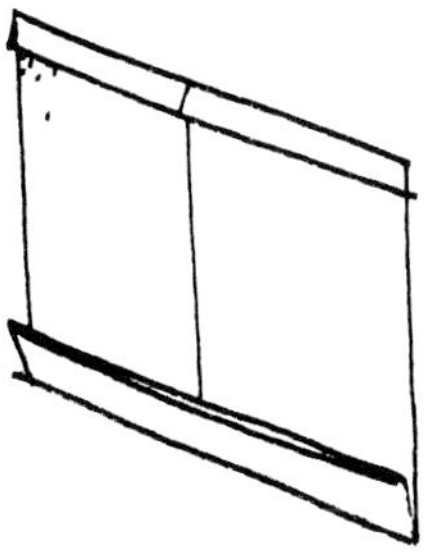

Fold up bottom

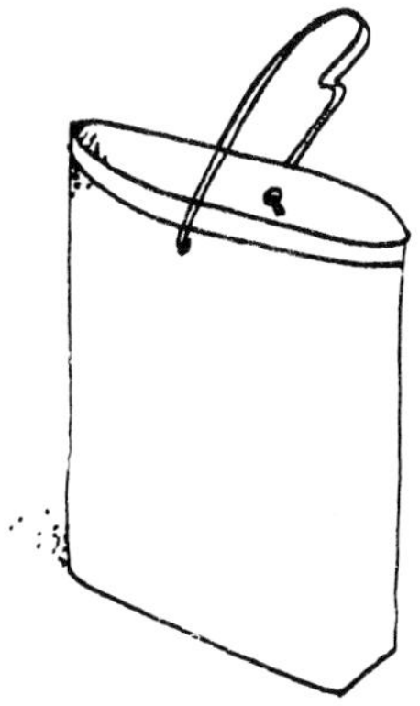

Open out bag, punch holes at top for ribbon

OVERPROOF
Frigate

Measuring Made Easy

How to Measure Liquids

METRIC	IMPERIAL	CUPS
30 ml	1 fluid ounce	1 tablespoon plus 2 teaspoons
60 ml	2 fluid ounces	¼ cup
90 ml	3 fluid ounces	
125 ml	4 fluid ounces	½ cup
150 ml	5 fluid ounces	
170 ml	5½ fluid ounces	
180 ml	6 fluid ounces	¾ cup
220 ml	7 fluid ounces	
250 ml	8 fluid ounces	1 cup
500 ml	16 fluid ounces	2 cups
600 ml	20 fluid ounces (1 pint)	2½ cups

How to Measure Dry Ingredients

15 g	½ oz	
30 g	1 oz	
60 g	2 oz	
90 g	3 oz	
125 g	4 oz	(¼ lb)
155 g	5 oz	
185 g	6 oz	
220 g	7 oz	
250 g	8 oz	(½ lb)
280 g	9 oz	
315 g	10 oz	
345 g	11 oz	
375 g	12 oz	(¾ lb)
410 g	13 oz	
440 g	14 oz	
470 g	15 oz	
500 g	16 oz	(1 lb)
750 g	24 oz	(1½ lb)
1 kg	32 oz	(2 lb)

Quick Conversions

5 mm	¼ inch	
1 cm	½ inch	
2 cm	¾ inch	
2.5 cm	1 inch	
5 cm	2 inches	
6 cm	2½ inches	
8 cm	3 inches	
10 cm	4 inches	
12 cm	5 inches	
15 cm	6 inches	
18 cm	7 inches	
20 cm	8 inches	
23 cm	9 inches	
25 cm	10 inches	
28 cm	11 inches	
30 cm	12 inches	(1 foot)
46 cm	18 inches	
50 cm	20 inches	
61 cm	24 inches	(2 feet)

Note:

We developed the recipes in this book in Australia where the tablespoon measure is 20 ml. In many other countries the tablespoon is 15 ml. For most recipes this difference will not be noticeable.
However, for recipes using baking powder, gelatine, bicarbonate of soda, small amounts of flour and cornflour, we suggest you add an extra teaspoon for each tablespoon specified.

Using Cups and Spoons

All cup and spoon measurements are level

METRIC CUP		
¼ cup	60 ml	2 fluid ounces
⅓ cup	80 ml	2½ fluid ounces
½ cup	125 ml	4 fluid ounces
1 cup	250 ml	8 fluid ounces

METRIC SPOONS	
¼ teaspoon	1.25 ml
½ teaspoon	2.5 ml
1 teaspoon	5 ml
1 tablespoon	20 ml

Oven Temperatures

TEMPERATURES	CELSIUS (°C)	FAHRENHEIT (°F)	GAS MARK
Very slow	120	250	½
Slow	150	300	2
Moderately slow	160-180	325-350	3-4
Moderate	190-200	375-400	5-6
Moderately hot	220-230	425-450	7
Hot	250-260	475-500	8-9

Index

Almond
chocolate steamed pudding 43
cream and chocolate flan 64
praline 73
Apricot truffles 86

Banana
boats 39
chocolate coupes 35
cream 44
Basic chocolate sauce 24
Berry cake, flourless chocolate 31
Beverages
chocolate liqueurs 47
chocolate thick shake 47
hot chocolate mocha 47
Biscuits
chocolate fudgies 17
chocolate Viennese 23
florentines 14
toscanas 11
Black Forest gâteau 51
Boxes, chocolate 83
Brownies, double chocolate chip 18
Butter icing, chocolate 24
Buttercream, chocolate 14

Cake
see also Gâteau
chocolate chestnut 22
chocolate chestnut ring 60
chocolate deluxe 8
chocolate layer 10
chocolate log 23
devil's food, with fudge filling 12
flourless chocolate berry 31
flourless mocha macadamia 17
honeycomb Siena 17
marble 12
pear and chocolate sponge 14
Vienna 11
whisky prune chocolate 43
Cakes
see also Slices
chocolate and coffee éclairs 58
chocolate cases 10
chocolate chip cookies 19
lamingtons 21
lucernes 21
profiteroles with rum sauce 58
Candy *see* Confectionery
Candy peel, chocolate, with Cointreau 82
Caramelised orange rind 42
Caraque 24
Cases, chocolate 10
Cassata, ice mountain 40
Castles, chocolate, with fudgy sauce 37
Charlotte
chocolate 34
maraschino 38
Cheese and chocolate bites 86
Cheesecake
chocolate 42
chocolate orange 32
Cherry liqueurs 78
Chestnut
chocolate cake 22
chocolate ring 60
creams 81
marron Mont Blanc 38
Chocolate chip
brownies 18
cookies 19
Choux pastry 58
Coffee
see also Mocha
and chocolate éclairs 58
chocolate liqueurs (beverage) 47
cups 28
hazelnut clusters 83
Cointreau chocolate mousse 33
Confectionery
see also Praline; Truffles
cherry liqueurs 78
chestnut creams 81
chocolate candy peel with Cointreau 82
chocolate cheese bites 86
chocolate delights 19
chocolate ginger 81
chocolate hazelnut 76
chocolate marzipan roll 83
chocolate peppermint leaves 72
chocolate peppermint shells 82
crunchy chocolate squares 81
Dale's delight 87
Easter eggs and chocolate boxes 83
hazelnut coffee clusters 83
marzipan 83
passionfruit creams 82
strawberry creams 87
white chocolate nut fudge 84
Cookies *see* Biscuits; Cakes
Cottage cheese and chocolate bites 86
Coupes
chocolate banana 35
coffee 28
tiramisu 43
Creamy chocolate sauce 24
Crêpes Tia Maria 28
Crunchy chocolate gâteau 55
Crunchy chocolate squares 81
Cupid's chocolate cake 55
Cups *see* Coupes
Custards, petits pots au chocolat 38

Dale's delight 87
Date fudge slice 11
Delights, chocolate 19
Deluxe chocolate cake 8
Devil's food cake with fudge filling 12
Dobos torte 51
Double chocolate chip brownies 18

Easter eggs and chocolate boxes 83
Eclairs, chocolate and coffee 58
Eggnog and chocolate flan 58

Flan
chocolate almond cream 64
chocolate eggnog 58
chocolate meringue 59
chocolate pecan pie 62
chocolate walnut, with orange pastry 62
mint chocolate 59
poire William chocolate 46
Florentines 14
Flourless chocolate berry cake 31
Flourless mocha macadamia cake 17
Fondant
boiled 70
fruit dipping with 75
simple 72
Fondue, chocolate rum 42
Fruit dipping with chocolate or fondant 75
Fudge (confectionery)
chocolate hazelnut 76
white chocolate nut 84
Fudge cake filling 12
Fudge date slice 11
Fudge sauce 37
Fudgies, chocolate (biscuits) 17

Gâteau
Black Forest 51
chocolate orange 50
chocolate ricotta 50
chocolate rum 52
chocolatine 54
crunchy chocolate 55
Cupid's chocolate cake 55
Dobos torte 51
ice mountain 40
mandarin surprise 50
marron Mont Blanc 38
mint chocolate 54
paradise ring 41
Sacher torte 20
sherry mocha dessert 36
Gelato pronto 34
Ginger, chocolate 81
Glacé icing, chocolate 24

Hazelnut
chocolate fudge 76
coffee clusters 83
truffles 79
Honeycomb Siena cake 17
Hot chocolate soufflé 46
Hot mocha chocolate 47

Ice cream, chocolate 39
Ice mountain 40
Icing
caraque 24
chocolate butter 24
chocolate glacé 24

Lamingtons 21
Layer cake, chocolate 10
Lemon coconut truffles 78
Liqueurs, cherry (confectionery) 78
Liqueurs, chocolate (beverage) 47

Log, chocolate 23
Lucernes 21

Macadamia mocha cake 17
Mandarin surprise gâteau 50
Maraschino charlotte 38
Marble cake 12
Marble pudding, chocolate 37
Marron Mont Blanc 38
Marzipan 83
chocolate roll 83
Mascarpone, chocolate and cream cheese strudel 63
Meringue chocolate flan 59
Microwave chocolate truffles 86
Mint
chocolate flan 59
chocolate gâteau 54
chocolate leaves 72
chocolate sauce 24
chocolate shells 82
Mocha
hot chocolate 47
macadamia cake 17
sherry dessert 36
Mousse, chocolate Cointreau 33

Nègre en chemise 46

Orange
caramelised rind 42
chocolate cheesecake 32
chocolate gâteau 50
and chocolate soufflé 44
chocolate trifle 35
pastry 62

Pancakes
chocolate walnut 30
crêpes Tia Maria 28
Paradise ring 41
Passionfruit creams 82
Pastry
choux 58
orange 62
rich shortcrust 62
sweet shortcrust 59
Pears
and chocolate sponge 14
Hélène 39
poire William chocolate tart 46
Pecan chocolate pie 62
Peppermint *see* Mint
Petits pots au chocolat 38
Pie
see also Flan
chocolate Pithiviers 63
Pistachio nut and port truffles 77
Pithiviers, chocolate 63
Poire William chocolate tart 46
Port and pistachio nut truffles 77
Praline 39
almond 73
chocolate cinnamon balls 87
powder 73
Profiteroles with rum sauce 58
Prune whisky chocolate cake 43
Puddings
see also Steamed pudding
chocolate castles with fudgy sauce 37

Rich chocolate sauce 24
Ricotta chocolate cake 50
Rum
chocolate fondue 42
chocolate gâteau 52
chocolate soufflé 35

Sacher torte 20
Sauce
basic chocolate 24
chocolate mint 24
creamy chocolate 24
fudgy 37
rich chocolate 24
Sherry mocha dessert 36
Shortcrust pastry
rich 62
sweet 59
Siena cake, honeycomb 17
Slice
date fudge 11
double chocolate chip brownies 18
Soufflé, chilled
chocolate rum 35
nègre en chemise 46
orange and chocolate 44
Soufflé, hot
chocolate 46
Sponge, pear and chocolate 14
Steamed pudding
chocolate almond 43
chocolate marble 37
Strawberry creams 87
Strudel, chocolate, mascarpone and cream cheese 63
Sweet shortcrust pastry 59
Sweets *see* Confectionery

Tart *see* Flan
Ten minute truffles 76
Thick shake, chocolate 47
Tia Maria crêpes 28
Tiramisu 43
Torte *see* Gâteau
Toscanas 11
Trifle, chocolate orange 35
Truffles
apricot 86
hazelnut 79
lemon coconut 78
microwave chocolate 86
port and pistachio nut 77
ten minute 76

Vienna cake 11
Viennese, chocolate 23

Walnut
chocolate pancakes 30
chocolate tart with orange pastry 62
Whisky prune chocolate cake 43
White chocolate nut fudge 84